famous
l o v e r s
in the Bible

famous
lovers
in the Bible

And Marriage-Building Secrets
We Learn from Their Relationships

Doug and BJ Jensen

new
hope
PUBLISHERS

Birmingham, Alabama

New Hope® Publishers
P. O. Box 12065
Birmingham, AL 35202-2065
www.newhopepubl.com

Library of Congress Cataloging-in-Publication Data
Jensen, Doug, 1952-
Famous lovers in the Bible : and marriage-building secrets we learn from their relationships / Doug and BJ Jensen.
p. cm.
Includes bibliographical references.
ISBN 1-56309-810-5
1. Married people in the Bible. 2. Marriage-Religious aspects-Christianity. I. Jensen, BJ, 1945- II. Title.
BS579.H8J46 2004
248.8'44—dc22
2003020159

ISBN: 1-56309-810-5

N044104 • 0104 • 11M1

dedication

To our wonderful son and daughter-in-love,
Jeff & Monica Morgan.

And also, with love and deep
appreciation, to Dad and Mom
Jensen, George & Cheryl Battung,
Randy & Linda Case, Doug & Jamie
Cummings, Bill & Pam Farrel, Brad &
Christy Fox, Ron & Mary Johnson,
David & Jeanie Lopez, and Mark &
Kirsten Strawn. We are grateful for all
your prayers, support,
and friendships.

Table of Contents

Preface

*W*hat couples come to mind when you hear the descriptive phrase *famous lovers*? Romeo and Juliet, Mark Anthony and Cleopatra, Scarlett O'Hara and Rhett Butler . . . or Kermit the Frog and Miss Piggy? The world remembers and records the dramatic stories of the lives of passionate *famous lovers* like these.

Passion enhances or destroys love relationships, especially marital relationships, depending on what or whom the individuals are passionate about. Some marriages fail for lack of desire or because a spouse directs attentions to objects or people other than the marriage partner. Yet, there are married couples who channel passion and cultivate love to such an extent that they create great marriages. What do these couples do to experience long lasting, devotion-filled unions?

We can't say that simply being a Christian ensures that you will have a terrific marriage, or even a marriage that lasts. Depending on how you read the statistics, the divorce rate in the US is either 1 in 2 or 1 in 4. But no less a reliable statistician than George Barna has found that the divorce rate for born-again Christians (27%) and fundamentalist Christians (30%) is higher than the rate for non-Christians (23%). God can enable us to be faithful and fulfilled marriage partners, yet so many Christians fall instead into the culture of divorce.

After two years of failing at marital satisfaction, instead

of heading to the divorce court, we decided to devote ourselves to the study of marriage building. Fifteen years of research later, we still believe there is no better resource than the Bible. All the knowledge needed for creating a more fulfilling marital relationship is found between the pages of Genesis and Revelation.

Since 1989, we have used the information we found to mentor and help married couples create stronger, God-centered marriages by using biblical principles. In the process of teaching others, our own marriage greatly improved. Imagine that!

In *Famous Lovers in the Bible*, we examine the lives of ten Biblical couples. All of the men and women were passionate—but not always for each other, and not always for the best reasons. By looking at the marriages of these ten couples, we discovered life-changing secrets. We learned from their positive examples as well as from their mistakes and applied the lessons to our own marriage. And it has worked for us! Our marriage keeps growing in love and intimacy. We hope you'll want to learn and apply the secrets of each biblical couple as we have, so you can build a stronger, God-centered marriage, too.

We have changed the names of people in the contemporary stories to ensure privacy. Besides, we know most of these couples personally and wanted to continue our friendships after this book was published!

We thank the couples who shared their stories, our editor Karen O'Connor and New Hope editor Rebecca England, and our fellow writers in the San Diego Writer's Guild for their input and encouragement.

—Doug and BJ Jensen

How to Use This Book

The most important thing you can ever do for your marriage is to accept Jesus as Lord of your life. Until you are a Christian, you can't understand God's perfect intention for marriage, because you haven't experienced God's perfect expression of love—His self-giving through His Son, Jesus Christ.

It isn't just knowing who God is and going to church that makes someone a Christian. Even Satan and the demons believe in God and shudder (James 2:19). Some people *put in their time* going to church, but do not have a personal relationship with Jesus. Going to church without putting Jesus first in your life and marriage is like standing on the right road but not moving in the right direction. Accepting Jesus as the Savior and Lord of our life moves us toward heaven.

If you are not a believer in Jesus, this is an invitation to you to ask Jesus into your heart right now. "If you confess with your mouth 'Jesus is Lord,' and believe in your heart that God raised him from the dead, you will be saved" (Romans 10:9). If you are a believer and your spouse is not (we know many couples in this situation), continue to pray for your spouse and invite them to church as often as the Holy Spirit leads you to do so. We know how your heart is aching. Be faithful in prayer because the prayer of a righteous person is powerful and effective (James 5:16).

Once we have this personal relationship with Jesus, we will desire to do His work (James 2:14–24). Then we need to make choices to help us continue on the path toward spiritual development and producing fruit in our marriages and for God's kingdom. Be proactive! Joyfully embrace the challenge and enjoy the journey.

There are 10 chapters in this book, each featuring a different couple in the Bible. Each chapter contains three sections:

- A section written by both Doug and BJ focuses on the predominant theme in the relationship of the famous lovers.

- A section written by Doug addresses the male in the relationship and a challenge he faced.

- A section written by BJ addresses the female in the relationship and a challenge she faced.

Marriage-Building Secrets: Each of the 30 sections is followed by a marriage-building secret to be learned from the biblical couple's relationship.

Discussion Questions: At the end of every chapter there are questions for discussion—either as a couple, or for a group if you use this book for group study.

famous lovers

Adam
and Eve

Genesis 1:26–3:24

The Once-Perfect Union

From BJ & Doug's Perspective

*a*dam shouted for joy when he first saw Eve, "The man said, 'This is now bone of my bones and flesh of my flesh'" (Genesis 2:23). Adam and Eve were *made for each other* . . . literally. Even though they had obvious differences, God had a plan in bringing them together. "And the two will become one" (Matthew 19:5), two unique individuals coming together to form one whole unit—God's perfect union.

Adam and Eve were blessed with the best circumstances. After all, they were surrounded by ideal conditions in the Garden of Eden. God Himself had supplied all their needs. Food was bountiful and delicious. Their work was stimulating and rewarding. They must have experienced pure, unabated joy, unconditional love, and complete companionship.

Adam and Eve had no tension, pressure, or stress. Time was on their side—there were no busy schedules to separate them, no mountain of bills to climb, no pile of emails to delete, no little ones running underfoot. We imagine that, from the moment they gazed into each other's eyes, each was passionate about the other and how wonderful life would be together.

Yet with every advantage, their union failed to live up to their Creator's expectations. What happened to wilt the promise? We know what happened in our marriage. Life happened. And God gave us freedom of choice. Unfortunately, we are imperfect human beings and have a propensity for making choices that can alter the most blissful of beginnings.

Creating a Joy-Filled Union

Great marriages don't just happen automatically. Those who are married know how challenging relationship building can be! But ordinary men and women have an opportunity to create an extraordinary marriage. Our success depends on our attitudes, behaviors, choices, and decisions.

To experience a great relationship like God intended, we need to construct our marriage from the Creator's blueprint. "'And the two will become one flesh.' So they are no longer two, but one" (Mark 10:7–8). Previously, we thought this meant a couple becomes one physically, but now we see it also means mentally, emotionally, and spiritually. Creating oneness between a male and female takes great effort.

A famous muscular actor said in an interview on television, "I work hard at the movie studio. I work hard at the exercise studio. I don't want to have to go home and work hard at marriage." He has been divorced several times. An unwillingness to work and an expectation of easy happiness can almost ensure failure in marriage.

Marriage building takes deliberate effort because God's plan for a perfect union includes:

- *Initiating* a personal relationship with God
- *Imitating* godly behavior
- *Inviting* God to be the head of your marriage

Initiating a Personal Relationship with God

One of the key ingredients in building a stronger marriage is acknowledging the creator of marriage, God, and developing an intimate personal relationship with Him. We have grown to know Him better each day by:

1. **Reading God's Word**—The Bible helps the invisible God become visible. When we immerse ourselves in His book daily, we get to know Him on a more intimate level. When we began to seek to know God better, we had a hard time understanding the King James Version. Thankfully, there were other translations, so we tried many. We like the New International Version, and our quotes in this book are exclusively from the NIV. Find a translation that speaks to you personally and immerse yourself in God's Word.

2. **Praying**—Prayer is simply talking with God. Any long-lasting, intimate relationship depends on consistent, quality conversation. The closeness of our relationship with God is directly proportional to the time spent communicating with Him. Keep a running conversation with God while driving, cleaning house, exercising, etc. When we spend time and energy developing our relationship with God, we experience the peace, love, and joy that comes from God's Spirit.

3. **Worshiping and praising**—Worshiping draws us into His world of love, peace, and joy. Praise fills our heart

until it bubbles over with gladness. Praising God gives us a greater appreciation for His qualities of compassion, grace, and mercy, and all He has done. Recognizing and appreciating what God has done for us prompts us to want to give back in return.

The Marriage Triangle Theory

As we develop a closer *personal* relationship with the God of love, we also draw closer and more loving to our spouse. As we draw closer to our spouse, the love in our marriage is elevated. To see how this theory works visually, take a look at the Marriage Triangle Chart:

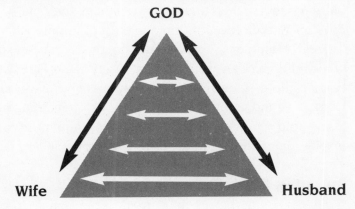

With God at the head of our marital relationship, we impact future generations as Grandpa and Granny Goody did. Farmers Grandpa and Granny Goody worked a small family homestead until their deaths at the ages of 96 and 94. Both publicly declared their acceptance of Christ as their Lord and Savior during their wedding ceremony in 1908. Back on the farm after their weekend honeymoon, Grandpa took seriously his new responsibility as the spiritual leader. He confidently and quietly stated to his new bride, "We will commence each of our married days spending personal time with Jesus."

Thereafter, at the crack of dawn, Grandpa bundled up, stoked the embers in the fireplace in the living room, and retreated to his quiet place in the barn. Upon rising, Granny headed to her weathered rocking chair in front of the warm fire. Each carried a worn Bible to their favorite place to meet with the Lord.

Prior to every meal, Grandpa read Scripture aloud and led prayers. Each night before climbing into their feather bed, Granny spent time holding Grandpa's hand and kneeling with him to give thanks to the Lord for all their blessings, even when times were tough. As their marriage developed, their love for God and each other intensified.

Their example spoke volumes to their children and grandchildren. They were a living legacy of St. Francis of Assisi's quote, "Preach the gospel always. If necessary, use words." Grandpa and Granny Goody's granddaughter, Mary, told us how her grandparents influenced and inspired her and the entire family in a profound way.

Imitating Godly Behavior

"Then God said, 'Let us make man in our image, in our likeness'" (Genesis 1:26). To create a perfect union, we need to reflect God's image. When we reflect, we are called to be a *mirror* for the God who created us, although our imitation of the Creator will at best only resemble godliness. We decided to personally do a better job of reflecting God's image by being more patient, forgiving, loving, and encouraging.

Reflecting God's ways calls for submission to Him. When Doug seeks God's will and spends time reading Scripture and praying each morning, I (BJ) notice a tremendous difference in his countenance. I think, *Wow, I want to be more loving and peaceful like that, too.* Reflecting the image of God leaves no room for self-agendas or self-sufficiency. It is a choice to imitate, reflect, submit, and act with a servant's heart.

Marie was one of many we interviewed when we sought advice from happily married couples. She had been married over 50 years at that time. "You cannot be selfish and be happily married, period!" Marie stated with authority. Selfish human passions blur the desired image of God. We need to seek God's guidance when we want to improve our marriage.

Inviting God to Be the Head of Your Marriage

God is the creator of marriage. He is the head, the one in charge, the Alpha and Omega, the boss, the commander, the CEO. He is the absolute authority. The buck needs to *go to* and *stop at* God's desk.

Adam and Eve were called to obey God. "And the LORD God commanded the man, 'You are free to eat from any tree in the garden; but you must not eat from the tree of the knowledge of good and evil, for when you eat of it you will surely die'" (Genesis 2:16–17). God told them the consequences of not being obedient. Only the One in highest authority has the right to command and set the consequences of failure.

We can choose to obey God or we can choose to live on our own terms. There will be rewards or consequences depending on our choices. I (BJ) learned the hard way in my first marriage. We lived life on our own terms and didn't pursue God. If it was convenient, we put in our time in church on Sunday. That marriage ended in divorce. Now, after marrying Doug, who takes his role as a

Christian husband seriously, I've experienced marriage both with and without God's leadership. No comparison.

God is a God of order and purpose. He has a plan but will not force us to follow it. It's our choice to acknowledge Him as the head of our marriage and personally choose to follow His incredible plan of unconditional love, grace, mercy, forgiveness, and productivity, or not. Personal ambitions are puny in comparison to the richness and fullness of life God wants to give us through our marital relationship. There is peace and joy to be found in letting God run our marriage. It's our choice to relinquish control to God and follow His leadership. "A cord of three strands is not quickly broken" (Ecclesiastes 4:12).

The Story of Adam and Eve

Adam was responsible for working in the garden and nurturing God's earthly creation (Genesis 2:15). Adam was also given the job of naming everything (Genesis 2:19). God was the one who noticed that Adam needed a partner, saying, "It is not good for the man to be alone. I will make a helper suitable for him" (Genesis 2:18). Out of all the animals he had created, a suitable helper for Adam was not found. So God put Adam into a deep sleep, took one of his ribs, and created a woman. Eve was designed to be Adam's helpmate. She was created to complement, enhance, and complete him. Eve was the completion of the whole unit of marriage. The woman was a gift to the man. It's so awesome to think of our mate as a *gift from God*. Adam and Eve's union was meant to be complete and permanent.

The Scripture then goes on to explain that the man declared that the woman was "bone of my bones and flesh of my flesh." Adam meant this literally, because God had created Eve from Adam's rib! The next verse explains how this relates to all other husbands and wives—they are to be united to each other, to be "one flesh."

So God created the first marriage and placed the man and woman in the Garden of Eden, where all their needs were met. They lived there in happiness and trust in God; the Scripture says, "The man and his wife were both naked, and they felt no shame."

**The secret
to creating a better union is . . .**
Initiating a personal relationship with God, Imitating godly behavior, and Inviting God to be the head of your marriage.

Temptation Enters
From BJ's Perspective

love what I learned from Eve's story of temptation. I call her story "the forbidden fruit fling that put Eve in an apple jam!" "Now the serpent was more crafty than any of the wild animals the Lord God had made. He said to the woman, 'Did God really say, "You must not eat from any tree in the garden"?'" (Genesis 3:1). When the serpent tempted Eve, he had a plan. Eve was naive and so are we if we think we can resist temptation by ourselves. That's when we're jelly in the tempter's hands.

Temptation is enticement to commit an unwise or immoral act, with a promise of reward. No one escapes being tempted or attracted to something that is not in God's will. Studying Eve makes me feel so vulnerable but causes me to take action to prevent being spiritually compromised like she was. She didn't see temptation coming.

The enemy will appeal to our greedy nature, desires for pleasure, and selfishness by whispering how good something will be, causing us to want something that is not in our best interest. "When you eat of it your eyes will be opened" (Genesis 3:5). Once Eve saw the delicious-looking apple, she *wanted* the forbidden fruit. She succumbed to temptation.

Satan, the master of deception, will disguise himself as our friend and appeal to our selfish nature. Jesus hadn't eaten for forty days when Satan tempted him to turn the stones to bread and eat. Jesus quoted Scripture to avoid giving in to Satan's temptations (Matthew 4:1–11).

Being tempted is not a sin. All of us will be tempted. Submitting to temptation is the sin because it separates us from God. But hope is not lost. We have choices. When Satan knocks at my door, I can invite him in, remain and entertain him, or slam the door in his face. *Praying* or *calling on the name* of Jesus helps me resist temptation and makes the devil flee (James 4:7).

Eve made at least three mistakes when she was tempted:

1. **She relied on herself.** Eve responded to temptation before seeking counsel. We all need help. We are too vulnerable and weak to battle the forces of evil alone. Facing a powerful adversary alone is a prescription for failure. Eve could have turned to God or Adam, who was standing right there. She didn't realize that:
   Sin will take you farther than you want to go,
   Keep you longer than you want to stay,
   And cost you more than you want to pay.

2. **She multiplied her sin.** "She also gave some to her husband, who was with her, and he ate it" (Genesis 3:6b). Beware! Sinners love company. Eve sinned and tempted Adam to sin. Was it so she wouldn't feel guilty? "Here, Doug, have a second helping of my delicious chicken lasagna even if you're full (and then I

can, too)." I'm no better than Eve, tempting my husband when I know it's not in our best interest. "Do not cause anyone to stumble" (1 Corinthians 10:32).

3. She covered up her deceit. Before sinning, Adam and Eve were comfortable in their state of nakedness. I doubt that Eve had any self-esteem issues. Adam did not lust after every other woman in the world. (Okay, so there weren't any other women—a mere technicality.) But when Adam and Eve sinned, they realized they were naked, were ashamed, and covered themselves up with fig leaves. There are consequences for disobedience. Because of sin, Eve and Adam went from living unashamed to feeling that they had something to hide or cover up. These two, who had enjoyed a close and trusting relationship with God, were now hiding in the bushes, avoiding God to keep Him from seeing their shame.

Sin Separates

When we sin as Eve did when she sinned (relying on self, multiplying sin, or hiding it), there will always be some adverse consequences. But God gave us assurance that we can turn away from temptation: "No temptation has seized you except what is common to man. And God is faithful; he will not let you be tempted beyond what you can bear. But when you are tempted, he will also provide a way out so that you can stand up under it" (1 Corinthians 10:13).

Sometimes we think the worst thing that could happen is for our sin to be exposed. Actually, the worst thing would be for our sin to remain hidden and to fester, grow, and intensify! Confessing our sin and bringing light into the darkness may be a shameful and painful experience, but it is the only way to seek forgiveness, reconciliation, healing, and growth.

**The secret
of handling temptation is . . .**
Seeking God's way out.

The Blame Game
From Doug's Perspective

As a man, I often find myself trying to fix problems, whether they're in me, my spouse, others, or in things around the house. My dilemma with the story of Adam and Eve eating the forbidden fruit is, "How does Adam fix, or un-eat, the fruit?" I compare eating the forbidden fruit with saying something negative to BJ. How can I take back hurtful words? It's like putting toothpaste back in the tube.

People love to be recognized for doing something good, honorable, or altruistic. In fact, sometimes I have gone out of my way to be sure others see what a wonderful thing I did, so that I will be recognized for my goodness. It's like telling everyone how humble I am. However, when I do something wrong, there seems to be no limit to the number of ways I try to hide or avoid responsibility for my actions.

Blame Begins Early

From the very first sin of the world, human beings have looked for ways to avoid responsibility for their bad choices. One day I was watching my preschool granddaughters play. I saw Nicole push Mandy, who landed with a thump on the floor and began crying. She picked herself up and ran to me for comfort. After holding her and drying her tears, I turned to Nicole. "Did you push your sister?" I asked.

"No," replied Nicole innocently.

"Nicole!" I said sternly.

Nicole justified herself immediately. "Mandy took one of my crayons."

After explaining to Nicole a more appropriate way of handling crayon rustlers, I reflected on the event. I marveled at how a four-year-old had already learned the fine art of avoiding responsibility by blaming. Nicole's response was classic.

How To Avoid Responsibility

The original pattern for blame was established by Adam and Eve. Thanks, you guys! We are still seeking to avoid responsibility for poor choices in three main ways. God can't be impressed with any of these:

1. **Concealing or hiding the wrongdoing.** "They hid from the LORD God among the trees of the garden" (Genesis 3:8). We think if we can hide our sin, that no one will know. God knows.

2. **Avoiding responsibility for the wrong by changing the subject.** "The LORD God called to the man, 'Where are you?' He answered, 'I heard you in the garden, and I was afraid because I was naked; so I hid'" (Genesis 3:9–10). Like Adam, I am tempted to hide my sin so I can avoid the disapproval of God and the inevitable consequences. And just like in Adam's case, it never seems to work for very long. The truth always becomes evident. "And [God] said, 'Who told you that you were naked? Have you eaten from the tree that I command-ed you not to eat from?'" God knew exactly what had happened, and He confronted Adam.

3. **Blaming someone else when sin is exposed.** "The man said, 'The woman you put here with me—she gave me some fruit from the tree, and I ate it.' Then the LORD God said to the woman, 'What is this you have done?' The woman said, 'The serpent deceived me'" (Genesis 3:12–13). When our granddaughter Nicole realized I had seen her pushing her sister, she no longer tried to convince me she had not committed the act. Instead, she blamed her sister. Why was it so hard for Adam and Eve to admit they had sinned and eaten from the tree? Why is it so hard for us to admit our sin?

When confronted with his sin of eating the forbidden fruit, Adam responded by blaming God and Eve—"the woman You put here with me." Nice going, Adam. Up to this point, there were only four intelligent beings—God, Adam, Eve, and Satan. Adam blamed two of the four. Why he left out Satan and himself is a mystery to me. Maybe he wanted to leave someone for Eve to blame.

Did Adam believe that God and Eve were actually responsible for his eating the fruit? If Adam thought like I do, the answer is probably yes. When it comes to wrong-doing, I minimize my own part and magnify someone else's part. It's the reverse of when something goes right. I magnify my own efforts, while often failing to recognize the important contributions made by others. Forgive me, Lord.

My Sin

Formerly, I believed it was better to hide my sin than to face the consequences. Before marrying BJ, I had developed a drinking problem. It was ruining my life, but other than that it wasn't a problem. I promised her that I would not drink after we were married. I was faithful for several months, but then I succumbed to temptation and began drinking again without her knowledge. I concealed this behavior for the first two years of our marriage and could have continued for many more.

However, I couldn't hide my sin from God. "The LORD searches every heart and understands every motive behind the thoughts" (1 Chronicles 28:9). "Oh LORD, you have searched me and you know me. You know when I sit and when I rise; you perceive my thoughts from afar" (Psalm 139:1–2). The Holy Spirit, whose job it is to confront us with our sin, was working on my heart.

The conflict within me became so great that I could no longer live with the duplicity. I came to the conclusion that I would rather face the consequences than continue lying. I asked for God's forgiveness and was assured of His pardon. "If we confess our sins, he is faithful and just and will forgive us our sins and purify us from all unrighteousness" (1 John 1:9).

I humbled myself and confessed to BJ. It was a very painful time in our relationship. She struggled to forgive because she felt deceived, betrayed, and hurt. With God's help, she forgave me, and with God's and BJ's assistance, I was able to stop drinking. The bumpy road of our marriage was patched and eventually improved in spite of this ugly pothole of deceit.

The Holy Spirit Convicts

When we sin, avoiding detection may seem like a victory, but two things will occur:

• The Holy Spirit will convict you of your sin.

• Satan will enlarge your sin and cause concealment to become more difficult and more painful.

God's Word provides a solution to the dilemma. "You will know the truth, and the truth will set you free" (John 8:32). I had to endure the consequences of my sin, which included rejection by BJ until her heart softened. But by telling the truth I no longer had to feel guilty, and I no longer had to live a lie to cover up my sin. I felt as free as a released prisoner of war!

The Biblical Model for Repentance and Forgiveness

God, in His wisdom, provided a solution to our challenge, but only after I admitted wrongdoing. The model of repentance and plan for restoring a broken relationship was presented in the parable of the lost son (Luke 15:11–32). The son demanded from his father his part of the estate, left home, and squandered his money in a foreign land.

After he hit bottom, he developed a plan of repentance, found in verses 17–20. There are three parts:

1. **He humbled himself.** The young man admitted his wrongdoing to himself and he was humbled. He even told his father he was unworthy to be called *son*. Our prideful nature tells us that we do not need to ask for forgiveness. It says we did nothing wrong, or our wrongs were minor infractions that do not require confession. Humility is accepting the fact that we are imperfect and that we make mistakes. A humble person would rather admit a mistake, learn from it, and reconcile a relationship. "Before his downfall a man's heart is proud, but humility comes before honor" (Proverbs 18:12). Unless we humble ourselves, it is very difficult to go on to the next step.

2. **He confessed his sin.** "Father, I have sinned against heaven and against you" (Luke 15:21). Confession puts the cards on the table for all to see. That is difficult. Confession of sin to a spouse is admitting a mistake, and we feel vulnerable. That is why humility comes first. We can ask God for the courage and strength to humble ourselves and confess the wrongdoing.
   After humbling self and confessing sin, ask God and the person you wronged to forgive you. If you are the spouse who is being asked to forgive, notice the example of the father, who ran with open arms to the returning son, eagerly acting to restore his son to full status. We can choose to forgive our spouse and be reconciled; to hate the sin but love and forgive the sinner.

3. He planned to work to repair the relationship. The young son, as he thought what he would say to his father, planned to repay his father for the damage done, saying "Make me like one of your hired men" (v. 19). His changed heart encouraged him to pay back what he could through hard work. Could he restore all that he had taken from his father? Hardly. Often when we hurt someone we cannot completely compensate for their loss. But the truly repentant person is not just asking for quick forgiveness—they show that they are willing to work to restore trust. The father, with his unconditional love, was so eager for reconciliation that he swept aside the son's protestations before he could utter them (see vv. 21–22). But the son showed his sincerity by asking for a chance to work at reconciliation.

Lessons Learned

If Adam had responded like the lost son, he may have said: "God, You created me to be perfect, yet I have let You down. Against Your instruction, I stood by while the woman You gave me ate the forbidden fruit, and then I ate some too. I cannot undo my actions, but please, God, tell me what can I do now to regain a right relationship with You."

I will remember the story of the prodigal son the next time I find myself with forbidden fruit in my mouth and I hear God asking, "What have you done?" Instead of hiding, denying, or blaming, I can choose to humble myself, confess my sin, and seek to restore a right relationship with God and my spouse.

**The secret
to ending blame is . . .**
Admitting when we are wrong and
asking forgiveness.

Questions for Discussion and Action

1. Of the three essential ingredients to creating a better marriage (*Initiating* a personal relationship with God, *Imitating* Godly behavior, and *Inviting* God to be the head of your marriage), which area do you need to improve in? What steps will you take?

2. What part of asking forgiveness from your spouse is most difficult for you and why?

3. What temptation do you deal with most frequently? What are you doing about it?

famous lovers

Abraham
and Sarah

Genesis chapters 12, 16, 20, and 22

A Story of Faithfulness

From BJ & Doug's Perspective

*T*he name Abram means "father." It must have been an embarrassment to Abram for 86 years to be called "father" when he had no children. God made a covenant with Abram and his family at the time He told him to go and live in Canaan. Later in Abram's life, God changed Abram's name to Abraham, "father of nations," when God made a covenant with Abram to give him a child who would have descendants as numerous as the stars in the sky.

Abram's wife Sarai's name means "my princess." She struggled and suffered for many years because she was barren, and had no children. When God renamed Abram as the "father of nations," He changed Sarai's name to Sarah, meaning "princess." She was no longer to be only Abram's princess. She became a princess to all and the mother of nations.

Faithfulness in Marriage

Abraham and Sarah are an excellent example of a couple who were faithful to each other and to God. The term covenant, as it is used in the Bible, means a binding promise made between God and man. Marriage is also a covenant. When we marry, we promise to be faithful not only to our spouse but also to God. Faithfulness to God is an important factor because it is impossible to be faithful to God and unfaithful to a spouse.

Abraham was among the many people in Hebrews 11 noted as being faithful to God. Abraham is mentioned in the New Testament more than 70 times, not because he was always a pillar of perfection, but because through testing he developed into a man of faithfulness.

Does God expect us to be completely faithful all the time? Solomon, the wisest of kings and writer of Proverbs, was convinced no man could be (Proverbs 20:9). However, Abraham and Sarah proved that even though we may fail on occasion, we can still grow into people of great faith.

Belief and Faith

Some people think believing in God is having faith in God. Not so. Justin and Marnie illustrate the difference between belief and faith.

While Justin pedaled the bicycle built-for-two, Marnie glided along behind. They were on a *whatever comes next* kind of adventure that some newlyweds find exhilarating on a Saturday. Their laughter and bantering came to a halt when they reached the entrance to a rickety hanging bridge. Was it possible that their weight on the dilapidated wooden-planked bridge would cause its collapse? The two dismounted to discuss their options.

"Do you think its safe to ride across?" asked Marnie.

"I believe so," said Justin, faking confidence.

Marnie questioned, "Do you believe it enough to get back on the bike and give it a go?"

Faith is a belief we hold on to and move toward with action. It is believing from a distance the bridge will hold you up and then moving across the bridge with confidence. As we trust in God's promises and experience their reality, we develop faith. "Now faith is being sure of what we hope for and certain of what we do not see" (Hebrews 11:1). "Without faith it is impossible to please God" (Hebrews 11:6). Faithfulness calls for belief and obedient action.

Beginning the Journey of Faithfulness

Abram did what God required. When God first called Abram to pick up and go to a different place, to leave his town and take his family to a new land, Abram was faithful, and unquestioning in his obedience.

Sarai was, too. She accompanied her husband to a foreign land even though it wasn't easy to be uprooted from family and friends. She didn't have the benefit of hiring *Camel Movers, Inc.* to help her pack. She couldn't contact AAA or MapQuest for detailed directions even if she suspected her husband wouldn't stop and ask for them along the way. There is no mention of Sarai arguing, balking at leaving Haran, or showing unwillingness to change direction in mid-life.

Abram, at age 99, was circumcised along with all the males of his family and household, as the Lord had commanded. His actions proved his faith and the Lord credited it to him as righteousness. Abram and Sarai believed in God's promises to the point of committing their lives and livelihood to God.

Abram and Sarai stumbled in their faith. On two separate journeys to foreign lands, Abram feared for his life. He told Sarai to lie and tell the Egyptians and King

Abimelech of Gerar that he was her brother rather than her husband. These were half-truths because Sarai was his half-sister. Later Abraham and Sarah laughed at God's promise that they would have a son when he was 100 years old and she 90, and that his heirs would number as many as the stars in the sky.

Abram and Sarai's faith was not perfect. They made mistakes and sometimes failed to fully trust God. That showed their humanness, but God loved them and continued to bless them because they persevered.

Another Test

Isn't it amazing that after their faithfulness had been demonstrated for years, God gave Abraham and Sarah another test? God instructed Abraham to take his long-awaited and beloved son Isaac to the region of Moriah. Abraham was to sacrifice Isaac there as a burnt offering.

It's almost impossible to imagine the horror Abraham and Sarah must have felt as God requested such a sacrifice. Isaac was the son they loved more than life itself. They would have gladly given their lives in place of Isaac's.

Sacrificing Isaac as a burnt offering was a test to see if Abraham and Sarah would be steadfast in the most difficult of circumstances. They were. Their faithfulness and obedience were rewarded when God spared Isaac's life. And yet the story of Jesus reminds us that God did not spare Himself. The story of Isaac reminds us of the incredible sacrifice God made in sending His Son Jesus to die for our sins.

Abraham and Sarah's story reminded us of a couple we know, John and Stacy, who also showed a willingness to sacrifice.

Faithfulness Rewarded

John and Stacy Dalton and their two young children lived in a spacious home in San Diego, surrounded by luxuries. Then they felt called by God to go to Southeast Asia as missionaries. After prayerful consideration, they quit their lucrative jobs, sold their home, packed a few personal belongings, and faithfully headed for a third world country for language training. Neither had ever been to Indonesia. It was a demanding transition. Here in California they had enjoyed the support of a large extended family. There, they didn't know anyone.

Their extreme sacrifice reaped great rewards. They loved the Indonesian people and the slower-paced culture, which provided time *to be*, not just *to do*. Both blossomed in their jobs: his was flying medical supplies to remote villages and hers was ministering to local women.

During a recent visit in the U.S., they had difficulty readjusting to the fast-paced lifestyle. They enjoyed spending time with loved ones in San Diego, but they couldn't wait to get back *home* to Indonesia where they could continue to serve God and enjoy His incomparable blessings.

God's Promises

God is always faithful to His promises (Psalm 145:13; Hebrews 10:23). He promised to give Abraham and Sarah descendants as numerous as the stars in the sky. He did. He promised to provide for all John and Stacy's needs if they would "seek first his kingdom and his righteousness" (Matthew 6:33), and then He blessed them beyond what they could imagine for their faithfulness. And He does the same for all of us when we step out in faith.

The secret
to faithfulness is . . .
Trusting in God's promises.

Obedience to God

From Doug's Perspective

Abraham was the leader of his family. He was responsible for setting a good spiritual example for his wife in his relationship with God. I am also required to set a good example for my wife and family. My ignorance of that job responsibility caused me to fail sometimes in the early years of my marriage. Now informed, I am trying to be more like Abraham and grow toward becoming a faithful and obedient spiritual leader of the family.

As parents, we want our children to be obedient. Sometimes we even demand that they obey us. If we see the importance of our children obeying us, why is it sometimes so difficult for us to obey our Heavenly Father? Obedience often has a negative connotation; perhaps it is because surrendering free will, independence, and control is not easy in our "me first" society.

Freedom Is Not Free

Engraved in the polished marble of the Korean War Memorial in Washington D.C. is the statement, "Freedom is not free." The events of September 11, 2001, reiterate that point. The privilege of freedom requires sacrifice.

The military is responsible for maintaining freedom overseas, and the police do the same within our cities. One distinction of both is the necessity that all who serve within the organization faithfully follow orders. Each member must strictly obey commands, even if it means their life. Men and woman give up their lives for our country because they believe that the country's freedom is more important than their own individual life. The secret to their obedience is humble surrender of their own will for the greater good of the whole.

Responding to God

Sometimes God asks us to trust His plan for our life, even when the circumstances seem impossible. I had to trust God to provide for my family for the years when my income was cut in half. I was impressed with my obedience until I heard Bob's story.

One summer, Bob was on a choir tour and staying at the house of a hosting church member. His hostess was a gracious widow in her eighties named Irene. On a shelf in her home, Bob saw a photograph of an elderly man. "Is that your husband?" he inquired.

"Yes, and we had three wonderful years of marriage."

"Did you marry later in life?"

"Oh no," she exclaimed. "Samuel and I were married forty years."

Bob was really confused. "If you were married 40 years, why do you say you had three wonderful years together?"

Irene explained. "When we married, I was a believer, Samuel was not. There were so many things that I wanted to share with him but couldn't. I prayed every day for 25 years that my beloved Samuel would become a believer. One day, I sensed God's assurance that he would, but it didn't happen right away, so I continued praying daily for twelve more years. Finally, Samuel came to believe that Jesus was his Lord and Savior. After that we had three of the most wonderful years of intimacy that any couple could hope for together before his death."

Help My Unbelief

I believe Irene was like Abraham. He believed that God was faithful to His promises, but as years passed and they had no children, unanswered prayer was getting hard to ignore. Irene, as well as Abraham, may have prayed, "I do believe; help me overcome my unbelief!" (Mark 9:23–24).

I relate to Abraham. I sometimes find myself asking God to bless *my* plan for my life. But that is not His way. God had a plan for Abraham's life and He has a plan for your life and mine. He does not change His plans. We are to be obedient to His plan. God challenged Abraham to continue trusting Him in spite of the circumstances. In God's perfect time, Abraham and Sarah had a son, Isaac.

No Lord, Not Another Test

Headlines could've read, "Faithful Man Endures 25-Year Test. Finally Rewarded." The birth of Isaac could have been a wonderful end to Abraham's story. But it wasn't.

Obedience to God sometimes requires us to go beyond what we think is humanly possible. Abraham was asked to sacrifice Isaac as a burnt offering. I can't imagine! After getting over the initial shock and horror, I suspect Abraham seriously questioned whether he had heard God correctly. But Abraham decided to obey God, even though what God was asking made no sense to him at the time.

After God commanded, Abraham left early the next morning, traveled three days, and then made two amazing statements that showed his humble surrender to God's plan. First he told the servants who had traveled with him to stay in camp while he and Isaac went on to worship. "We will worship and then we will come back to you" (Genesis 22:5). Note the second *we*. I think Abraham was confident that he would return with Isaac alive. Secondly, as they traveled up the mountain Isaac asked, "The fire and wood are here . . . but where is the lamb for the burnt offering?" Abraham answered Isaac, "God himself will provide the lamb for the burnt offering, my son" (Genesis 22:7–8).

These verses show Abraham's total trust and obedience to God's plan. How could Abraham know that everything would end well? He knew God was faithful to His promises. God promised to produce nations, kings, and rulers through Isaac, therefore Isaac would not die. Abraham could make these two statements with confidence. Abraham learned the secret to obedience: humbly surrendering to God's plan and trusting that God is faithful to His promises.

Obedience Rewarded

Paul beautifully expressed to the Philippians the concept of obedience and God's reward:

"Your attitude should be the same as that of Christ Jesus: Who, being in very nature God, did not consider equality with God something to be grasped, but made himself nothing, taking the very nature of a servant, being made in human likeness. And being found in appearance as a man, he humbled himself and became obedient to death—even death on a cross! Therefore God exalted him to the highest place and gave him the name that is above every name." —Philippians 2:5–9

God rewards those who humbly surrender in obedience to Him. Jesus was rewarded with the highest place in heaven, given the name that is above all other names, and given authority over all things. Abraham's obedience was rewarded with a son and the certainty that his descendants would be as numerous as the stars in the sky. Our obedience to God in our marriage will be rewarded when we humbly surrender our will to Him and trust in His promises.

**The secret
to being obedient is . . .**
Humble surrender to God's will.

Waiting for God's Perfect Timing

From BJ's Perspective

There is more Scripture written about Sarai/Sarah than any other woman in the Bible. She wasn't perfect, but she did set an example for all wives on how to be faithful and desire God's will for her husband and her marriage.

When introduced to Sarai, we are told she is the wife of Abram and that she was barren (Genesis 11:29-30). Quite a way to introduce someone! Barrenness was a humiliation. It was one of the biggest disgraces in her day because infertility had a stigma attached; it meant God did not favor the woman or her marriage. It is certain that Abram and Sarai were both deeply saddened because they had no children.

God loved Sarai and wanted to grant her deepest desire—to bear a child. He had greater plans for her than she could ever imagine, but Sarai needed to wait on God's perfect timing. She could have used more patience. Sarai felt that her biological clock had all but wound down. Her Energizer batteries were drained. Time was definitely not on her side anymore!

Sarai's story confronts many contemporary wives. We're an impatient bunch, too. Living in a microwave mentality society, we want things to happen instantly, or better yet, yesterday.

After years of not conceiving, the once mild-mannered Sarai blamed her infertility on the Lord. She decided to take charge. Sarai told Abram to sleep with her maidservant Hagar to build a family through her. Abram agreed to sleep with Hagar. When Hagar conceived, she flaunted her pregnancy and Sarai experienced pangs of vicious jealousy. I'm not sure what Sarai expected, but she certainly got more trouble than she bargained for when she took things into her own hands.

Sarai lamented to Abram, "You are responsible for the wrong I am suffering. I put my servant in your arms, and now that she knows she is pregnant, she despises me." She's blaming Abram for the misery he brought on her! Can you believe a wife would do such a thing? Oops—been there, done that.

When God told Abraham and Sarah they would have a son, it was welcome news after many years of infertility. One major problem: it sounded unbelievable to the elderly Sarah that she would be the mother. But she desperately wanted it to be true. Sarah believed her husband was to become the "Father of multitudes," and in her barrenness she longed to be a part in making that happen. Her faith was being tested and she was proving to be faithful. So does her story continue smoothly? Of course not—it's real life!

In the barren or desert times of our life, we have difficulty imagining circumstances could be any different. It's confusing to know what to do and what not to do to change undesirable situations. Sometimes we get in trouble by taking matters into our own hands and not waiting for God's help or His perfect timing. While we are waiting, we could read Scripture, pray, and pour our heart out to Him (like Hannah did in 1 Samuel 1:1–20).

Sarah finally became pregnant. Sound the trumpets— it's a boy! She bore a son to Abraham when she was 90 and he was 100. They named him Isaac, which means *he laughs*. I can just see the wrinkles from years of worry replaced with joy lines. Isaac was the key ingredient in the fulfillment of God's promise to Sarah, and he arrived at the very time God promised.

When I think of Sarai's tribulations before Isaac was born, it reminds me of Beth's story.

Beth and Tom

Beth and Tom had a passion for children but were also barren for the first seven years of their marriage. Impatience caused heartache. A dark cloud hovered over their relationship and strained their marriage. Pleading for insight, they asked God why He wasn't allowing them the one thing they so desperately wanted—a child.

They undertook procedures for in vitro fertilization, but $30,000 later there was still no pregnancy, so they considered adoption. Beth heard about a single mom who had given birth to twins and planned to have them adopted. Their knowledge as attorneys helped speed up the process of adopting the infants.

In California, birth parents have up to one year to sign adoption papers. Six months after they took the twins into their home, the twins' biological father reentered the scene. Their dream unraveled faster than a ball of twine in a kitten's paws. The court awarded custody of the twins to the natural father.

After months of grieving their loss, Beth and Tom were given a second chance with another set of adoptable twins. They felt confident because both birth mother and father signed necessary papers to relinquish custody. But unbelievably, within the year these babies were also reclaimed by their birth parents.

Years later, Beth and Tom heard about the plight of unwanted orphans in Romania. Feeling God's strong urging, they flew to Romania and adopted a young brother and sister who became a double blessing to them. Both Beth and Sarah experienced God's perfect timing.

Whose Timing?

Compare Sarai's story to Elizabeth's in Luke 1:5–25. She, too, was old and barren, but rather than invent her own plan, Elizabeth waited patiently on God's timing and continued to pray for a child. When she gave birth in her old age, she thanked God for the son who would grow up to be John the Baptist.

Too often, I make my life miserable when I take things into my own hands. Like my first marriage, which was totally my idea and not God's. Bad move. Or doing what I want before praying about what God wants. Everything works more smoothly for me when I pray and wait on God's perfect timing.

**The secret
of waiting on God's timing is . . .**
Developing patience and trust
through prayer.

Questions for Discussion and Action

1. Scripture reading, prayer, and worship will help you develop a stronger faith. Which of these areas do you need to put more time and energy into?

2. Why is obedience to God important in marriage? What steps will you take to personally develop more obedience?

3. In what ways has personal faith in God impacted and improved your marriage relationship?

CHAPTER 3

famous lovers

Isaac and Rebekah

Genesis 24; 25:19–34; 26; 27

When Love Fades

From BJ & Doug's Perspective

Isaac may have been in his teens when his father Abraham took him to Mt. Moriah to be offered as a sacrifice. Although the young Isaac would have been physically stronger than his elderly father, he allowed Abraham to tie him and place him on the altar. Isaac was the epitome of an obedient son, and he learned a valuable lesson because of it. God protects and rewards those who obey.

As a teenager, Rebekah was a generous and compassionate person. When a stranger at the well asked her to give him water from her jar, Rebekah not only gave him a drink, but she offered to draw water for his camels, too. Talk about hospitable and hard working. Drawing water from a well was a laborious chore, let alone drawing *and* carrying enough water to fill troughs to quench the thirst of ten bottomless camels!

Rebekah also graciously offered the stranger and his traveling companions a place to stay for the night. She was outgoing, friendly, righteous, generous, compassionate, energetic, hard-working, and hospitable.

When Isaac and Rebekah met, she was polite and proper, he was obedient and respectful. Isaac married Rebekah because of his father's wishes, and he lovingly cared for her. These two famous lovers brought some impressive qualities to their marriage. But unfortunately, those excellent qualities, as well as their love for each other, diminished and they didn't live happily ever after. Similarly, the love faded in our next couple's story.

Stan and June were a strikingly handsome, well-dressed, sharply groomed couple who attended a couples' workshop we were leading. They seemed to have everything going for them. We liked them immediately—they laughed at all our jokes! While listening to them talk during a break, we quickly realized they were struggling in their marriage.

"We're here because Stan and I don't know each other anymore," June said.

Stan added, "Things changed after our son and daughter were born. Providing for their needs pulled us in different directions. I spent more time at work. She spent her time catering to the kids. There was less and less time for *us*. Now, the kids are away at college and we hardly know each other. It's been almost 20 years since we devoted any quality time to each other exclusively."

Fading Intimacy

We could relate to Stan and June because we too had drifted apart in our own marriage. Work obligations, parenting issues, and extracurricular activities pulled us in different directions. The intimacy of Isaac and Rebekah, Stan and June, and us imperceptibly deteriorated when the spouses devoted themselves to different priorities. Attending to many interests outside our marriage, we eventually felt love and companionship ebbing away. It is easy to get side-tracked from the marital relationship while raising children, doing work projects, hobbies, ministries, or other passionate interests. All can be valid pursuits depending on the amount of time spent. We learned that when we say "yes" to a good thing, we might be saying "no" to a great thing, like the intimacy in our marriage. When we finally realized these worthy activities robbed us of valuable relationship building time, we decide to purposefully schedule time together.

Time with children must be balanced with time alone together. A counselor shared with us: children are temporarily entrusted to us by God for 18 years or so, and then we are to lovingly release them into the world. If our partnership becomes less than fulfilling due to lack of maintenance during the child-rearing season, we may cling to our kids to fill the void. If we continue to nurture our marital relationship by keeping it a high priority, we can let go of our sons and daughters with joy.

What Can We Do?

Isaac and Rebekah's relationship teaches us two important lessons for building intimacy into a marriage. We see by their example it is beneficial to pray for your spouse and spend quality time with each other.

Pray for Your Spouse. Isaac and Rebekah knew it was beneficial to take their problems to the Lord. Isaac loved Rebekah even though she didn't bear him any children in their first 20 years of marriage. He felt helpless but showed his concern by praying for her. Rebekah turned to God during her difficult pregnancy when the babies seemed to be waging a war within her.

When a spouse is having difficulties at work, or physical challenges, or spiritual battles, we can always pray for them. We feel encouraged knowing our partner is praying for us. One way to initiate intercessory prayer for a spouse is to discuss the day's activities at breakfast. That way we are informed of activities or meetings that may require prayer support. We say simple prayers for each other throughout the day. These "prayer darts" keep us spiritually connected when we are physically apart.

When we feel separated from our spouse because of some minor misunderstanding, when we feel estranged from our partner, angry, or have just quarreled, prayer works. The Power Of A Praying Wife and The Power Of A Praying Husband, by Stormie Omartian, and Wives In Prayer, by Tami Chelew, are books that give structured help to people wanting to develop that skill.

Some of our arguments were resolved when we finally humbled ourselves and prayed together like this: "Lord Jesus, we have made a mess of this and we can't agree on what to do. Help! Forgive us for insisting on our own way. Grant us wisdom, direction, and peace." When we listened and waited for God's inspiration and peace to fill our hearts, our hearts softened and we asked each other for forgiveness. Then we were back on the road to oneness. What a blessing prayer can be for our marriage when we choose to pray with and for our spouse.

Spend Time with Your Spouse Even though Rebekah and Isaac respected and loved each other and were personally connected to God, their love faded and their relationship deteriorated. How could this happen? Maybe the shirts a couple at our church wore can give us a clue. On one side of Deanna and Dave's t-shirts was, "Know Fear."

On the other side, "Have Twins." First Isaac and Rebekah's relationship was tested by not having children. Then it was doubly tested by having twins! When children enter a family, a new dynamic is created. It becomes challenging to keep the marriage relationship a top priority.

When difficulties plague us or our spouse, we are often left feeling frustrated, helpless, or emotionally separated. But adverse conditions can actually be an opportunity to grow closer together by taking time to talk about the thoughts and feelings evoked. Getting in touch with and appropriately expressing our thoughts and feelings places couples on the same team looking for a solution together. Statements we have made like, "I feel so overwhelmed by all the responsibilities," "I feel unsupported in my decision," or "I feel disorganized when the house is a mess," can be springboards to clearer understanding of your spouse's needs. We don't try to fix each other's feelings; we just take time to listen. Then we discuss possible changes that can help satisfy the needs of both of us.

Some couples with children say they don't *have* time to talk with their spouse on such an intimate level because of the demands of child-rearing. We know others who have successfully kept the marriage flames burning while raising big families because they *take* time to be together. Let's look at what some couples are doing.

Pam and Jim decided to retreat to their bedroom three times a week for time alone to communicate. They scheduled this precious time to talk without interruption from their five children. Their kids learned not to interrupt Mom and Dad's time together unless they needed a ride to the hospital.

Mark and Kirsten purposely rise earlier than their four children each morning, go into their huge master bedroom walk-in closet, and pray together. This helps them feel connected and fortified for the busy day. When Mark is at work and Kirsten spends her day shuttling kids to different schools and activities, they remember to send up *prayer arrows* for the other person. They would rather be "sleep-deprived" than "God-deprived."

Jeff and Monica, who have three children under the age of 6, take time each morning to read daily devotionals together at breakfast.

Jamie and Doug have taught their children to play quietly in their own bedrooms until 7 A.M. That way Mom and Dad can have time alone with God and time to mentally plan their day.

The **Smyths** and the **McDonaldsons** are two families that enjoy spending time together. Because parents need time alone, they regularly reciprocate babysitting. It's an enjoyable break for the kids as well as for the parents.

Building Intimacy

You may be thinking, *Sure it sounds good to plan and spend some quality time together, but life challenges seem to constantly push us apart.* Building mental, physical, and spiritual intimacy is a continuing process that takes time and effort. Our friends Mary and Ron seek out relationship-building workshops, personal growth seminars, and couples' retreats yearly. We highly recommend scheduling regular getaways for just the two of you every three to four months. Couples we know swap babysitting duties with other trusted couples from church or in their neighborhood. Weekly date nights are a priority for us. When one of us reads relationship-building books, we share with our spouse what we learned.

It's essential to purposefully invest time and energy together in continually refueling our love relationship—especially through the child-rearing season. We remind ourselves that children are with us for a short time while a spouse is with us for a lifetime. Okay, 18 years may not seem like a short time to some of you. But for those of us who have grown children, the time seems to have passed quickly. Time devoted to the marriage is well worth the investment. And remember to connect when both of you have energy. Don't set aside your least productive time for your most important earthly relationship.

Modern Parable

A certain married couple were both entrepreneurs. They invested their life savings into a fledgling business. They loved and nurtured its development and were rewarded for their dedication. The business thrived. It proved to be so lucrative, they decided to diversify. Over time, they invested all their time and energy into five new enterprises spun off the original business. Spending day and night building each new business into a self-sufficient productive corporation, they one day realized the original business was bankrupt.

It's not about *having* time for a marital relationship once children come into the family. It's about *taking* time for the marriage. Spending time alone together is a choice. It can be scheduled in a DayTimer. If we aren't committed to making it a top priority, it won't happen.

Building intimacy into our marital relationship is a

challenge. We procrastinated for years before we realized we had to be proactive in developing our love relationship. The main point is that a plan needs to be made and purposefully implemented.

**The secret
to producing a strong love
relationship is . . .**
Continually investing in it.

A Man of Prosperity

From Doug's Perspective

God prospers (blesses) people in different ways. For instance, Isaac was blessed with a large inheritance, extensive land, and two sons. Isaac's grandson Joseph was blessed with power and influence as he ruled Egypt. John the Baptist was blessed with the Spirit of God and a mission to baptize many, even Jesus. Just as each of these men were blessed by God in different ways,

God also had a different plan for each man to follow, so that he could receive the blessing especially prepared for him. Have you ever thought about how you have been blessed with prosperity through God's plan for your life? Joe hasn't.

Whose Plan?

Joe was following a plan. Not God's plan, but rather a plan of his own making. This is what I know of Joe's story.

The cashier at the convenience store rang up the total for the six-pack of beer and five lottery tickets. "That will be $8.59."

Joe reached in his pocket and pulled out a tangle of dollar bills, but realized he didn't have the total amount needed. "Great," Joe muttered under his breath. "Just give me the six pack and four tickets." As he walked out of the store, Joe thought, I *had enough money last night before I went to bed. Sheri probably stole it from my dresser this morning before she left for work.* As he reached into his pocket for his car keys, he discovered the missing dollar bill.

Later that night in his apartment Joe told his buddy Ryan, for the hundredth time, that he *had* to win the lottery so he could quit his stinking construction job and start having some fun in life. Joe then yelled, "Sheri, I told you to bring each of us another beer. Get to it, woman. The lottery results are about to be announced!" The two men stared at the TV screen as the numbers were revealed. That night, in more ways than one, there would be no winner in Joe's house. As Sheri brought the beer, Joe grabbed it from her and raged, "That stupid clerk at the 7/11 kept the winning lottery ticket. I had five and had to give one back because somebody stole money off my dresser."

Some time later, Joe actually did win twenty million dollars in the California lottery. In talking privately to his buddy Ryan, I learned Joe made some changes. He quit his job, divorced, and bought a million-dollar house. I wondered if his good fortune brought him happiness.

The day I met Joe, I was appraising his 6,000 square-foot mansion. He never stopped complaining about the high cost and poor skills of the people who were remodeling the house. It seemed strange to me that he never smiled. I thought people wanted to win the lottery so they could buy anything they wanted and be happy. There was no prosperity in Joe's heart. He had monetary wealth, but he was still poor in spirit.

Do you know others like Joe who complain about everything and think they would be happy if things were different? They lament about wanting more money or a better job or boss. They complain about wanting to be married, or not married, or married to someone else. Some grumble that life would be better if they had a better vehicle, more free time, fewer obligations, or whatever.

Where Does Prosperity Come From?

Does prosperity come from attaining material things? Jesus said, "Watch out! Be on your guard against all kinds of greed; a man's life does not consist in the abundance of his possessions" (Luke 12:15). True prosperity is having a heart full of love, joy, and peace. God promised us prosperity—provided we accept His plan for prosperity in our lives. Jeremiah 29:11 says, "'For I know the plans I have for you,' declares the LORD, 'plans to prosper you . . .'" God wants to bless each one of us, and He does not need a lottery ticket to accomplish it because He knows lottery winnings will only give us money, not true prosperity.

Receiving God's Blessings

Do you know what God's planned blessing is for your life? Isaac made four decisions that allowed him to receive God's planned blessing for his life:

1. He trusted that God wanted to bless him and make him prosperous.
2. He was at peace with God's plan for his life.
3. He believed adverse circumstances of his life would not prevent God from blessing him.
4. He gratefully accepted the blessings God gave him.

1. Isaac trusted God's word. Isaac lived in the land of Abraham until a famine forced him to move. He moved with Rebekah and his whole household to the land of the Philistines. Once he arrived, God said to him, "Stay in this land for a while, and I will be with you and will bless you. For to you and your descendants I will give all these lands and will confirm the oath I swore to your father Abraham" (Genesis 26:3). If I were Isaac, I would have struggled to believe this promise because the circumstances of Isaac's life appeared contrary to God's design.

God promised to give him land that was occupied by the Philistines, a powerful, domineering people. Isaac had only himself and his own household in a scary foreign country. He lived in fear of his life because he thought the Philistine men wanted to kill him and take his beautiful wife Rebekah. Like his father, Isaac lied and told the king that his wife was his sister. But even though he was afraid, Isaac trusted God's promise and stayed in the land because he believed God was faithful to His word.

2. Isaac was content with God's plan for his life. How could Isaac be content if he was in fear for his life? Even though Isaac was fearful, he trusted that God would be faithful. Faithfulness allowed him to be content with God's plan.

God delivered Isaac from his fear. One day the Philistine King Abimelech looked down from a window and saw Isaac caressing Rebekah. Coincidence? In our house we would call it a *God-incident*. Why? Because God sometimes works through the circumstances of our lives to accomplish His will. The king summoned Isaac and found out Rebekah was really his wife. The king decreed that if anyone molested Isaac or Rebekah, they would be put to death. In this way God made it possible for Isaac and Rebekah to live in peace in the land. Once this happened, the next year's harvest turned out to be a record crop. Isaac continued to follow God's plan for his life and God continued to bless him.

Sometimes fear can be a good thing. It encourages us to trust in God and not ourselves. Or, fear may pressure us to change our situation because of the uncomfortable circumstances. There were times in my life when I changed professions because I was fearful, discontented, or uncomfortable with my work situation. It led me to change direction.

Other times I have tried to change but could not. Perhaps God was preventing me from changing jobs in those instances because He wanted to bless me where I was. God has a plan for our lives and God doesn't change His plans. When I stopped making plans based on my circumstances and sought His plan for my life through prayer, Bible reading and study, and surrounding myself with mature Christian advisors, I began to be blessed in many ways. BJ and I were blessed financially, with greater stability, and with more peace in our marriage. She was no longer concerned I would pursue some hare-brained scheme for making money or investments in a shaky stock market. Contentment with God's plan for me increased my job satisfaction and allowed me to experience joy in all my responsibilities as a husband, father, and grandfather. It took awhile, but I finally learned Isaac's secret of success—find and be at peace with God's plan for your life.

Isaac trusted God would bless him, and God did. "The man became rich, and his wealth continued to grow until he became very wealthy. He had so many flocks and herds and servants that the Philistines envied him" (Genesis 26:13–14).

3. Isaac believed God would bless him in spite of adverse circumstances. Have you ever been on a roll in life and then got slammed to the ground? If so, you can understand what Isaac experienced. There was Isaac, minding his own business, doing what God told him to do, getting blessed to the hilt, and then trouble started. The Philistines stopped up Isaac's wells so that his family and herds would have no water. King Abimelech, who had come to his rescue earlier, told Isaac to move out because Isaac was as powerful as the Philistines. It is amazing to me how quickly God blessed Isaac to the point of being as powerful as a whole kingdom.

Isaac made a wise decision to stick with God's plan. He knew God had promised to give him and his descendants the land, so he moved a little way away from King Abimelech and reopened the wells that had been closed up by the Philistines. He also dug two new wells, which the local townsman claimed should be rightfully theirs, so Isaac moved farther and dug another well. Isaac never got bogged down in worrying about these setbacks, because he trusted God would bless him in spite of adverse circumstances.

4. Isaac gratefully accepted God's blessing. We teach that "accepting graciously completes the act of giving." Isaac's decision to gratefully accept God's blessings was fully rewarded. After years of well stoppages, arguing over water rights and land, and fear of the Philistines, God appeared to Isaac and said, "Do not be afraid, for I am with you; I will bless you and will increase the number of your descendants for the sake of my servant Abraham" (Genesis 26:24). Shortly after that, King Abimelech made a treaty with Isaac. From that day to his death, Isaac lived in peace in the land God gave him.

**The secret
of prosperity is . . .**
Discovering and gratefully accepting God's plan
for your life and marriage.

Preventing Disconnection

From BJ's Perspective

*D*oesn't Rebekah's dilemma sound like a repeat of her mother-in-law, Sarah's? They shared the same personal heartache—barrenness. Even today barrenness causes a tremendous amount of marital strain. Many women in this situation feel pain, guilt, and judgment in not being able to fulfill their God-ordained role. These feelings could cause separation in the marriage.

Perhaps it was the 20 years of agonizing over not being able to conceive that caused Rebekah's character and personality to change so dramatically. Perhaps it was *having children* that created the change in her. Of all the admirable qualities we first observed in her at the well, none seem to be evident after marriage or childbearing.

Rebekah's Mistakes

I became aware of my own shortcomings when I observed Rebekah's marital and parenting skills. I made some of the same mistakes she did. With my new awareness of how things work to keep people connected, maybe I can refrain from repeating them in my marriage and with my precious grandchildren.

Some of the mistakes Rebekah made that caused disconnection from Isaac are:

1. lack of communication with her husband
2. concealing information from him
3. showing favoritism
4. deception

1. She didn't totally communicate. Rebekah had trouble telling her husband what was on her heart and mind. Can anyone relate? When Doug and I were faced with not being able to have children, we didn't talk about the feelings it evoked. We withdrew from one another mentally, emotionally, and physically. It increased our anxiety. Too often, when couples face unmanageable emotional issues, one or both emotionally separate rather than deal with the extremely uncomfortable feelings they are experiencing.

Doug withdrew mentally by working late. I learned to escape physically by running into the bathroom and locking the door to cry alone. Trial and error taught us these options didn't bring about the connection we so desperately needed at that time.

We were taught by a marriage counselor that a more connecting way is to be open and honest about thoughts and feelings than to ignore or try to escape them. It was difficult to get in touch with and share feelings that were triggered by uncomfortable situations, but continually working toward that goal eventually proved to be rewarding.

Validating a partner by saying things like, "I can see how you'd feel that way," or "You are so right," went a lot further to help the situation than, "You shouldn't feel that way," or "Get over it." Affirming a partner's strong feelings and grief can also be shown with hugs or statements like, "You don't deserve that," or "I'm sorry you're going through this right now, what can I do to help?" We worked through problems quicker when we didn't judge, minimize, invalidate, criticize, or isolate.

Unfortunately, Isaac and Rebekah don't seem to have understood the importance of total communication when feeling estranged. But after 20 years, God showed Rebekah mercy. She became pregnant. There was great rejoicing in her heart, but the joy was short-lived because her pregnancy was difficult. Was it a sign of difficulties to come?

It was admirable that Rebekah turned to God in her discomfort (Genesis 25:22). Did she learn that strategic behavior from observing Isaac? My husband has shown me the importance of spending time with the Lord. First thing every morning, Doug prays and reads the Bible. I hadn't been as diligent as he in making this a priority. When I witnessed the benefits of a close morning walk with the Lord by his example, I followed. I felt more connected to God, my spouse, and to my commitment to our marriage. I was more at peace and felt fortified to tackle the giants that came my way during the day. I believe it was honest communication with God that led me to honest communication with my husband.

2. She concealed information. When God told Rebekah, "Two nations are in your womb, and two peoples from within you will be separated; one people will be stronger than the other, and the older will serve the younger" (Genesis 25:23), she kept that information to herself. It was doubtful this information helped ease her physical pain, but it could ease her mental anxieties. It puzzled me there was no account of Rebekah sharing this pertinent word from the Lord with Isaac. We're talking about withholding a divine revelation! Why?

It was easy to judge and condemn Rebekah until the Holy Spirit convicted me. Early in our marriage I enjoyed shopping. Sometimes I spent more than I knew I should, so I'd withhold that information from my husband. I stuck new outfits in my closet until the newness wore off. After a few months, I'd wear the outfits. Doug would ask, "Is that new?" I'd innocently reply, "This old thing?" (Note to hubby: I don't do that anymore, honey! Honest.) I've withheld inspirations I've gotten during prayer times, thinking my husband would not believe me or would question my sanity. Or perhaps I questioned my own. Either way, I was just as guilty as Rebekah.

Withholding information is *not* productive. It is a form of deception and disconnection. It does not build the solid truthful marriage I seek to build.

3. She showed favoritism. The firstborn, Esau, was red and hairy. His fraternal twin brother, Jacob, followed closely behind. Esau grew up and became an outdoorsman, skillful in hunting. Jacob hung around the tents. Isaac loved Esau and his manly qualities. Rebekah loved the quiet son Jacob. I wonder if she showed him favoritism because of God's revelation to her, or maybe it was because she and her son had similar dispositions. Whatever the reasons, each parent blatantly embraced a favorite son.

Can you picture Isaac saying to Jacob, "Why can't you be more like your older brother and learn to hunt and fish?" Perhaps Rebekah vocalized to Esau, "Why can't you be more like your younger brother and learn how to cook and help out around the tent?" My aunt once asked me, "Why can't you be like the rest of the women in the family and learn to sew?" This was very hurtful to me.

Comparing siblings unfavorably or showing favoritism skews self-images, as it did for Jean. Jean was the second daughter in a home where the parents selectively loved and favored the firstborn. Her older brother was the recipient of all his parents' affection and attention. They spent more time with and listened more to her brother. Jean was constantly compared unfavorably to her sibling. This continual neglect and withholding of approval eroded her self-image and caused her to feel rejected and unworthy.

Her childhood baggage was carried detrimentally into marriage. Until she decided to change the self-image created in childhood, her marriage relationship was affected adversely. Instead of seeking self-worth from others, she decided to seek God's image of her. Her present marriage is thriving.

4. She deceived. Isaac was more than a hundred years old and blind. Fearing he was close to death, he wanted to give his blessing to his favored firstborn son. Rebekah overheard Isaac telling Esau to hunt some wild game and prepare a tasty meal for him, so that he could give Esau the blessing.

Rebekah devised a plan of her own. She cooked the requested meal and told Jacob to serve Isaac so he would receive the blessing and inheritance instead of Esau. I don't know if it was favoritism, her own selfish motives, remembering God's words, or just plain deception at work. Jacob balked at the idea and worried that Isaac would not be deceived. Rebekah insisted; she disguised

Jacob to feel and smell like Esau. She blatantly taught her son how to deceive. How sad. Do we do this? Have you ever told a child to lie and say they were a younger age to get a meal for a cheaper price, or a lower admittance rate to the movie? We damage our children when we teach them to deceive.

Jacob didn't want to betray his father or bring down a curse on himself, but he obeyed his mother. Dressed in clothes Rebekah stole from Esau, and with goatskins on his hands and neck so that he would feel like his hairy brother, Jacob approached his father. The plan to deceive Isaac worked and Jacob received the full blessing, along with the curse of being a deceiver that would plague him the rest of his life. The good news is we are never too old to change our ways.

Rebekah's Transformation

It was disheartening for me to see the vivacious, beautiful, generous, compassionate, hard working, and hospitable Rebekah transformed into a non-communicative, scheming, deceptive, disconnected wife and parent. Rebekah grew to regret her mistakes, poor choices, and inappropriate parenting techniques. Jacob had to move far away from home to avoid being murdered by his angry brother, and Rebekah never saw her favorite son Jacob again. Harsh consequences.

All too often, the consequence of poor communication, withholding information, favoritism, and deception is estrangement. With each mistake Rebekah made, these famous lovers drifted farther apart physically, emotionally, and spiritually.

> **The secret
> of staying connected in marriage is . . .**
> Communicating fully, frequently, and truthfully
> with your spouse.

Questions for Discussion and Action

1. If love has been fading in your marriage due to other commitments, identify them. What will you do to make time together a priority?

2. How have you been seeking God's plan in your life? In your marriage?

3. Is there a subject that you do not discuss in your marriage because you have uncomfortable feelings? Pray about ways you can raise the issue safely, and then communicate with your spouse.

famous lovers

Jacob and Rachel

Genesis 27–35; 37

A Love Story

From BJ & Doug's Perspective

*D*oesn't everyone love a love story where couples live happily ever after? Whether it's a young man dropping to one knee to propose wedded bliss or a great grandpa slowly bending over to kiss his wife's white-haired head as he rolls her in a wheelchair, these scenes bring warmth to our hearts.

Jacob passionately loved Rachel at first sight. But his passion for her didn't guarantee their marriage would run smoothly. Quite the opposite happened. What was it that allowed Jacob to continually love Rachel all of their days together?

His father Isaac advised him to take a wife from the family of Laban. Jacob traveled three weeks to reach the land where Laban lived. He stopped at a well and inquired, "Do you know Laban?" Shepherds at the well responded that Laban lived close by. While they were talking, Rachel, Laban's younger daughter, arrived with her father's sheep. "When Jacob saw Rachel daughter of Laban, his mother's brother, and Laban's sheep, he went over and rolled the stone away from the mouth of the well and watered his uncle's sheep. Then Jacob kissed Rachel and began to weep aloud" (Genesis 29:10–11).

Jacob was smitten from the get-go. Jacob's strength of passion, gratitude, relief, and conviction when his eyes feasted on his cousin Rachel is substance for a passionate story. But that's not the best part of this love story.

One month later Jacob asked Laban for Rachel's hand in marriage. Any modern day father might be shocked but appreciative if a prospective suitor asked for permission to marry his daughter. Check out Jacob's proposal: "I'll work for you seven years in return for your younger daughter Rachel" (Genesis 29:18). Seven years? That's 2555 days! Jacob could be nominated for giving the best proposal of all time. But that's not the best part of this love story.

Jacob completed seven years of labor for Laban, and then he announced, "Give me my wife. My time is completed, and I want to lie with her" (Genesis 29:21). That's getting right to the point! Remember, Jacob had been in Laban's fields for seven years, in the sweltering heat of the day and frigid nights, dreaming about his wedding night. He was anxious to claim what had been promised to him. But that's not the best part of this love story.

Laban planned a big wedding party for the whole town. Everyone ate, drank, and became merry. The celebration proceeded smoothly until Laban contrived a bait and switch trick. "But when evening came, he took his daughter Leah and gave her to Jacob, and Jacob lay with her" (Genesis 29:23).

Genesis 29:25 describes the surprise the next day: "When morning came, there was Leah!" Shocked, Jacob said to Laban, "What is this you have done to me? I served you for Rachel, didn't I? Why have you deceived me?" The deceiver had been deceived! Sometimes Scripture does not explain things in detail, and we're left speculating. How was it Jacob didn't recognize that Leah had been switched for Rachel? Jacob had been dreaming of this moment for seven years, and he was passionately in love with Rachel. Was it *that* dark? Was he inebriated from celebrating his marriage? Was he *that* anxious?

Laban shrugged it off by saying it wasn't the custom to give the younger daughter in marriage before the older one. He wanted Jacob to finish Leah's bridal week and then Jacob could marry Rachel in return for another seven years of work. This man drives a hard bargain! He finished the week with Leah, and then Laban gave him his daughter Rachel to be Jacob's wife.

Now read this carefully, because *this* is the best part of the love story. Because of Jacob's passionate love for Rachel, he was willing to work another seven years for her hand! Can anyone top fourteen years of labor for the privilege of marriage?

Even though there is no Scripture that states that Rachel returned Jacob's love (and she at times really tried his patience), he remained steadfast in his love for her to the end. We know this because when Rachel died, Jacob set up a pillar for her. Jacob only set up four pillars in his life: two to God on the two occasions when God appeared to him, one as a peace offering to Laban, and one for Rachel at her death. Jacob was faithful to his marriage promise to Rachel.

The worst part of the story is that Jacob wasn't loving toward his first wife, Leah. Leah suffered the humiliation of unreciprocated love. She felt her husband's rejection because Jacob made a decision not to love her. Are you married to someone you have decided not to love?

Another Love Story

The light chestnut horse approached the jump with confidence. Buck was a fearless American Thoroughbred with years of training in both cross-country and stadium events, and his rider was an experienced competitor. During the Memorial weekend event, no one was prepared for Buck's sudden stop, least of all his rider. Flying head first over the "W" jump, Christopher landed on top of his head, breaking his neck between the C1 and C2 vertebrae. It was the worst immobilizing spine injury possible. He couldn't breathe on his own.

After five days of unconsciousness, Christopher Reeve awakened in ICU. He was told by doctors that he had sustained a neck-down paralyzing injury. When the horrible realization was fully absorbed, he wanted to die and save everyone a lot of trouble.

His wife, Dana, came into the room. She stood beside Christopher's bed, and they made eye contact. Christopher mouthed his first lucid words to her: "Maybe we should let me go." Dana cried and said, "I am only going to say this once: I will support whatever you want to do, because this is your life, and your decision. But I want you to know that I'll be with you for the long haul, no matter what." Then she added the words that saved his life: "You're still you. And I love you."

If she had looked away or paused or hesitated even slightly, Reeve later said, or if he had felt there was a sense of her being noble, or fulfilling some obligation to him, he didn't know if he could have pulled through.

Wedding Vows

Have you ever experienced the challenge of keeping your wedding vows? We have. Being imperfect humans, we regretfully catch ourselves doing and saying things to each other that are hurtful. Regrets have a way of building up over a period of time. That's when a spouse doubts if she or he married the right partner. It's behavior like this that shows us why we need marriage vows.

Our vows are not only promises to our partner, they are also promises to God. They are pledges made to God about our commitment. The Bible is quite clear that vows must be fulfilled. "When a man makes a vow to the LORD or takes an oath to obligate himself by a pledge, he must not break his word but must do everything he said" (Numbers 30:2). "When you make a vow to God, do not delay in fulfilling it" (Ecclesiastes 5:4). For many couples, living out their wedding vows and commitment to each other becomes challenging. That was the case for Matt.

Commitment's Challenge

Matt's shoulders drooped and his back ached from another physically demanding day of construction work. As he opened the front door he speculated on who would be there to meet him. He knew he'd be greeted by his two wonderful children, but he was never sure if he would be welcomed by his wife, Kelly. Would she be there, or would it be Susan in a rage, or Cathy withdrawn and silent, or Linda obsessing over every little imperfection in the house? Matt took a deep breath and entered tenuously, hoping today would be different.

Kelly had been battling multiple personality disorder for years. When they looked at Kelly, family and friends saw a woman who had progressively lost her sense of reality and drifted into a dark, bottomless pit of oblivion. Matt saw the radiant bride he had married. Every day Matt reminded Kelly that God loved her and had a purpose for her life. He held stubbornly to the hope that some day she would again embrace life with energy and purpose.

Later that evening, after putting the children to bed, Matt still faced the same scene that had played out every night for two years. Kelly was catatonic, passed out on the living room sofa, from the battle that raged within her. Matt repeated his usual pattern. Lovingly and gently he picked her up, carried her to bed, and cuddled beside her. He would wrap his body securely around hers like a spoon.

In the morning he rose, made breakfast for his children and wife, and left for the construction site before anyone else was awake. At work, one of his co-workers asked, "How much longer are you going to endure your hopeless marriage situation?"

Matt replied with determination, "When Kelly and I exchanged wedding vows, I committed to God and to her that I would love her 'in sickness and in health.' I will honor that commitment. As long as I love her, the situation is not hopeless."

Through God's grace, Matt's steadfast love, praying friends, and the help of trained counselors, Kelly gratefully returned from her pit of despair. Today, she speaks to women about overcoming shame, guilt, and regret from difficult circumstances in their past.

Matt is a godly man who refused to see his wife through the clouded eyes of the world. He focused on the beautiful woman God created. Matt was committed to a marriage that would go the distance.

What allowed Matt to love Kelly through her darkest days? Was it his deep love for her? Yes, and more. It was his commitment to his marriage vows made not only to Kelly but also to God, to love her in sickness and in health, for better or worse. Matt was committed to keeping his vow, even if Kelly was incapable of responding to his love. Matt was determined to love her no matter what she did or how she responded because Matt was a man of passionate love and commitment.

**The secret
of a lifelong, loving marriage is . . .**
Commitment to your wedding vows.

Deceiving a Deceiver

From Doug's Perspective

Jacob's first big deception was pretending to be his older brother Esau so he could receive the coveted blessing from their father Isaac. In those times a father's blessing was like a will or trust of today. It passed on an inheritance, typically to the oldest son. By stealing the blessing Jacob believed he was obtaining an inheritance of vast lands and power. It backfired because Jacob was forced to leave the land he loved to avoid Esau's wrath.

God saw what Jacob did and was not pleased. Deceit is always a sin because it prevents full disclosure of the truth. Anything that hides even a portion of the truth is deception, which separates us from God. Jesus said "I am the way and the truth and the life" (John 14:6). It is His nature to always tell the whole truth. The truth is the way that leads to life.

The Source of Success

In exile, Jacob headed east. God appeared to Jacob in a dream and said, "I am the LORD, the God of your father

Abraham and the God of Isaac. I will give you and your descendants the land on which you are lying" (Genesis 28:13). No pun was intended by God, I assume, when He referred to Jacob "lying." This Scripture is highly significant. In my opinion, God was saying to Jacob, "I am the one who promised your grandfather Abraham and your father Isaac that their descendants would inherit the land. Therefore, do not deceive anyone, because I am the one who will bestow what I have promised. You wanted your father's blessing because you believed the blessing was a guarantee you and your descendants would inherit the land, but it is not your father's blessing that will make it happen. I am the God of success and I will make it happen."

Jacob had not trusted God with the outcome, so he stole the blessing. After God appeared to him, Jacob's heart was softened and he made a vow that he would trust God in the future, provided God continued to give him success.

My Vow of Honesty

When I was 12 years old my father caught me in a lie. I promised never to lie to him again . . . but I did. Then as an adult, I found myself lying to my employer, saying I was sick or at the law library to do some research, when I was actually going to a bar to get drunk. When I married I was determined to be truthful, but my thought process had not changed. I still believed it was better to lie and avoid immediate consequences than tell the truth and trust God to help me work through the consequences of my sin. I believe Jacob was like me, wanting to trust God by telling the truth, but being afraid God could not or would not help because of my past lies.

Jacob's Next Test

Twenty years after vowing to trust God, Jacob was faced with another test presented by his father-in-law. Laban was Jacob's match when it came to trickery! Jacob was stuck working for Laban beyond the agreed fourteen years, and Laban was not giving him anything for it—he was cheating Jacob out of his wages. Hmmm . . . looks like what goes around comes around. And around and around and around, as we witness in Jacob's life (see Proverbs 26:27 for God's version of this saying). Jacob had a decision to make. Would he allow Laban to continue to take advantage of him, or would he use deception to even the playing field? Would he trust God with the outcome and confront Laban, or would he revert to his previous deceptive ways?

Jacob took what he thought was the easy way out and deceived Laban. Not once but twice, first by secretly creating a large herd of his own goats from Laban's flock, and then by running away from Laban, taking with him Leah, Rachel, and their children, without even allowing Laban to kiss or say goodbye to his daughters and grandchildren.

Why was Jacob unable to confront Laban and tell him he was leaving? Did he not trust Laban? More than that, he didn't trust God to produce a good outcome if he was truthful. Jacob failed to act in faith based on his knowledge that God was more powerful than Laban. Laban discovered Jacob and his family had left, so he pursued and caught up to them. There were a few tense moments, but God was true to his promise to take care of Jacob. He warned Laban in a dream not to say anything to Jacob that could cause a fight. Laban chose to listen to God and let Jacob continue his journey home.

Three times Jacob had chosen to lie rather than trust God's promise to take care of him. Jacob's return to his homeland was an opportunity to change his ways and make honesty a habit. Unfortunately, this famous lover never found the courage to change. In his reunion with Esau, Jacob made statements that appeared deceptive. He also tried to hide the rape of his daughter Dinah from his sons. Deceit continued to be an ongoing life issue for Jacob.

Life Issues

A life issue is one that continually reappears in an individual's life. Typically it exists because we are not handling it in a way that pleases God. So God, in His infinite wisdom, repeatedly presents us with opportunities to handle the issue in a godly manner.

God gave Jacob many opportunities to be truthful and honest, but Jacob failed to see the importance of truthfulness. The most devastating part of not confessing, confronting, and conquering a life issue with God's help is that the issue may be passed on to the next generation, along with the pain, anguish, and shame that result from sin.

After the rape of Dinah, Jacob's sons killed all the men in the guilty man's city as revenge. Jacob's sons had not shared that plan with their father, which caused him great anguish because he feared a reprisal from other cities in the area.

The anxiety Jacob felt because of this incident was the size of a flea's whisker compared to the heartache brought on by the scheming deception of his ten oldest sons later in life. Jacob had given his favorite son Joseph a special multi-colored robe, demonstrating his special love toward Joseph. The other brothers were jealous, so when an opportunity developed, they kidnapped Joseph and sold him to slave traders headed for Egypt. Then they dipped his coat in goat blood and brought it to their father Jacob. Scripture depicts the excruciating anguish felt by Jacob. "He recognized it and said 'It is my son's robe! Some ferocious animal has devoured him. Joseph has surely been torn to pieces.' Then Jacob tore his clothes, put on sackcloth and mourned for his son many days. All his sons and daughters came to comfort him, but he refused to be comforted. 'No,' he said, 'in mourning will I go down to the grave to my son.' So his father wept for him."

Does Jacob's grief tear at your heart? Perhaps God was grieving too, not just for Jacob and not just for Joseph, but also for all the sons who learned the art of deception from their father.

Releasing the Pain

Like Jacob and his sons, all of us run the risk of passing down to the next generation sinful behavior that we fail to remove. When this happens there is still hope, as seen in this next story.

A large, barrel-chested man stood up at the men's seminar. With voice quivering and tears dripping down his cheeks, he said, "My name is Lou. I'm here tonight because I need to forgive my dad. He was an alcoholic who was absent every Christmas of my life. He ruined my childhood. I hated my dad for his drinking and I vowed as a child to never forgive him. My dad is dead now.

"I have a son here with me tonight, Derek. Even before Derek was born, I became an alcoholic. I missed Christmases with Derek because of my drinking, and I hated myself for that. My son has every right to hate me. But I don't want to go to my grave as my father did without getting things straight with my son." He begged the seminar leader, "Can you help me?"

The leader observed, "Your failure to forgive has held you in bondage. You can be released from the hateful feelings if you forgive your father tonight. It makes no difference whether he is here in this room or not. Would you like to forgive your father now?"

Lou choked out the words, "Yes. I forgive you, Dad."

The leader then questioned the son, "Derek, how do feel about your dad and his drinking?"

Derek, a boy of about 15 years, replied, "I thought I hated my dad for his drinking, but now I realize I just hate his drinking and not him."

"Would you like to forgive your father now for his drinking and how that has impacted your life?"

Derek did not hesitate. He turned to his father, hugged him, and said, "Dad, I forgive you."

Overcoming a Life Issue

Like Jacob, lying for me had become a way to get what I wanted and avoid uncomfortable confrontations. It also separated me from God, built barriers between me and BJ, and laid a heavy burden of guilt and shame on my soul. One day, by God's grace, I finally decided I was willing to risk the pain of truthfulness to release the pain of deception. I was amazed to discover that the pain of truth was less and lasted a shorter period of time. The pain of deception is long lasting and never seems to recede. BJ appreciates my honest approach to communication—but sometimes questions my truthfulness. That hurts, but I view it as God's way of holding me accountable.

Now, whenever I am tempted to tell a lie, I remember my past pain of deception and the horror of Jacob and Lou passing down a life issue—a sin—to the next generation. I know there will be repercussions from any fessing-up of untruthfulness, but I know God promised to be with me so I can trust Him with the outcome.

**The secret
of truthfulness is . . .**
Telling the truth and trusting God
with the outcome.

Jealousy and Discontentment

From BJ's Perspective

Rachel was a girl who had a lot going for her throughout her life. The Bible tells us she was "lovely of form and beautiful." Since her father Laban had two daughters, and Rachel was the younger, she was elected to the lowly position of shepherdess. She may be the only female sheep watcher who was mentioned in the Bible, so that told me she was unique. When cousin Jacob from a distant land came into her life, her future started looking brighter. He was searching for a wife, and he was smitten by her outer beauty.

Lasting relationships do not usually depend on physical attraction alone. The older I get, the more I realize how true this statement is. Mom warned me, get to know the *character* of a prospective mate and his parents. Getting to know someone's family and character takes time and observation.

Blind Passion

Having studied Rachel's character, I suspect she was a passionate person, but also a lamenter. Rachel may have been passionate, but her passion was not directed toward her husband. When she married, her tune was, "If only I had children to raise . . . then I would be content." She was fervent about having children. When Leah produced four sons by Jacob, Rachel could not contain her cool. Jealousy raged because Rachel was not able to conceive. She insisted Jacob sleep with her maidservant Bilhah (Genesis 30:3). Jacob obediently slept with Bilhah and she became pregnant—twice—bearing two sons. Was Rachel finally satisfied? Nooooo. Can you hear her continued plea of discontent, "If I had my *own* son . . . then I would be content."

In the meantime, in Rachel's self-imposed Olympic race for bearing sons, Leah and the maidservants racked up a total of 10 points. Women with sons in their society were honored with higher social status. I can understand if I had a background as a lowly shepherdess, I'd probably seek to raise my social status and gain higher esteem in my community. Even after Bilhah bore two sons, Rachel was not satisfied and pleaded with Jacob, "Give me children, or I'll die!" (Genesis 30:1).

"God remembered Rachel; he listened to her and opened her womb" (Genesis 30:22). Rachel gave birth to a son. But was she finally content that she had gotten what she wanted? I'm afraid not. She named her son Joseph, which means, "may he add" (Genesis 30:24). Before the blood on the body of her newborn baby was cleansed, Rachel was bemoaning again. This time it was something like, "If only I had another son . . . then I would be content."

With a blind passion for wanting sons, Rachel's discontentment became insatiable. Rachel had the love and devotion of a husband who was passionate about her and who gave her great material wealth, and yet it wasn't enough. Aren't we like that so often, continually wanting whatever we don't have? A bigger house, a better car, a higher social status. What a sad lot we can be—wanting what we don't have.

Later, Rachel conceived a second time. When it came time to deliver, she had great difficulty. As she was struggling to give birth, the midwife said to her, "Don't be afraid, for you have another son." Rachel named him Ben-Oni ("son of my trouble") and died. Ever hear the saying, "Be careful what you pray for?" Little did Rachel know at the time that she would die during childbirth, bearing the last of Jacob's sons. Rachel's discontentment led to an unsatisfying lifetime of competitive childbearing and discouragement.

Gratitude?

Do you think Rachel could have lived a longer, more satisfying life instead of continually agonizing through discontent? Not once are we told that she thanked God for her blessings or sought His will or plan for her life. I know as I draw closer to God and gratefully accept all He has given me, I am much less stressed.

Our precious granddaughter Nicole taught me a lesson in acceptance when she was five years old. I was discontent and complaining about my appearance one day. Nicole's childlike wisdom set me straight. "Mema, God made you the way He wanted you. You should be happy!"

**The secret
of contentment is . . .**
Acceptance.

Questions for Discussion and Action

1. What promises did you make to your spouse and to God on your wedding day? How well are you keeping yours?

2. Which of these three do you struggle with the most: jealousy, coveting, or envy? How does that affect your marriage?

3. How has speaking the truth to your spouse helped or hindered your relationship?

CHAPTER 5

famous lovers

Samson and Delilah

Judges 13–16

Obsession Concession

From BJ & Doug's Perspective

*S*amson had a passion. Unfortunately it was not a passion for serving God or fulfilling God's plan for his life. His obsession was women. The pattern of his life was foreshadowed in his first words recorded in the Bible when he spoke disrespectfully to his parents: "I have seen a Philistine woman in Timnah; now get her for me as my wife" (Judges 14:2).

Intermarriage or any sexual relation with Philistines was detestable to devout Israelites. Samson's parents tried to dissuade him, but he was insistent. He married the Philistine woman, but the relationship was short-lived. He sought other female conquests, among them Delilah, another Philistine, whom Samson found intoxicating.

Delilah was also passionate. However, neither God nor Samson was the focus of her hunger. Her obsession was the accumulation of personal wealth. When she was offered a large reward to discover the secret of Samson's superhuman strength and betray him to the Philistine rulers, she greedily complied. Samson and Delilah's worlds revolved around the unholy 'M' trinity: Me, Myself, and My.

The Focus of Obsessions

An obsession can be described as an addiction, compulsion, craving, drive, or dependence. When our mind is so totally driven by our desires, we are not able to submit to God and follow His plan for our marriage. An obsession pulls our focus off *selfless thinking* and holds us captive in *selfish thinking*. When we have an obsession, we are conceding a portion of our life to that obsessive activity rather than being fully devoted to our marriage.

Samson did whatever he pleased. In short, he was selfish. He wanted to lay with Delilah, so he did. Delilah was willing to give him what he wanted in exchange for what she wanted—information about his strength. She was selfish and conniving, too. Their obsessions dueled. He won the first three battles but she won the war.

Obsession in Our Marriage

During our wedding, we vowed to "love and cherish" each other. BJ believed that included spending time together, especially on the weekends. Doug believed it included doing things together, except Saturday, Sunday, and Monday night when football was on television. BJ decided to love Doug by letting him watch football until he had his fill although she questioned Doug's love for her. It appeared he loved football more than he loved her. After all, she thought, we spend our free time with the people and things we love most, right?

This challenge exists in millions of marriages. What is the answer? Should the wife concede and let her husband do whatever he wants? Should the husband concede and stop doing his favorite activities on the weekends? Should a compromise be negotiated? No one answer is right for every marriage. Every couple must make their own decisions. But we do know a breakdown of the relationship is possible, perhaps even likely, if obsessive behavior is not addressed constructively. Just look at the strain it placed on Samson and Delilah in their relationship.

Breakdown in Trust

These famous lovers utilized the compromise approach. He wanted to make love with her but she required something in exchange. Samson had to tell her the secret of his strength. She wanted to get rich by turning Samson over to the Philistines, but he wanted her body in return. Three times he teasingly mocked her by lying to her. However, her strong desire to collect the reward promised by the Philistines intensified her pursuit. She honed nagging into an art form. Like Chinese water torture, Delilah's insistency, consistency, and persistency finally wore down Samson's "resistency." Finally she said, "How can you say 'I love you' when you won't confide in me?" (Judges 16:15).

Their obsessions led to a breakdown in communication and the trust between them was destroyed. Samson tried to restore the relationship by telling the truth about his strength. This delighted Delilah. She used the information to betray him and thus ended their relationship—a relationship that showed the effects of obsessions allowed to run their course. It was similar for the following couple.

Admitting the Problem

Carole and Brandon were obsessed with different things. She loved to calm her nerves with food and developed an eating addiction. Brandon loved sports and obsessively played on four softball teams in the spring and summer, and three basketball teams in the fall and winter, plus the pick-up games of touch football in between. Whenever Brandon was off playing sports, Carole was eating because of loneliness. The larger his wife blossomed in size, the more time he chose to spend away from home. When he wasn't playing sports, he was watching them on television or getting together with friends to talk sports. That led Carole to eat out of frustration. The dynamics this created in their relationship pulled them in opposite directions. When they sought a Christian counselor they discovered the unhealthy dynamics, and the strain on their relationship caused by their obsessions. Carole and Brandon, Samson and Delilah needed to change. Too bad Samson and Delilah didn't seek godly counsel.

Choosing to Change

Through BJ's direct communication with Doug, he eventually realized that 12 hours of watching football every week could be considered obsessive behavior. Her approach was very loving. First, she spent some time with Doug as he watched football, sitting next to him on the couch and reading a book. Then she brought him chips, dip, and a drink so he could enjoy the game more. Finally, she would quietly go off and do something she wanted to do. After several months of this she inquired, "Could we go to the park this Sunday for a picnic?"

"There's a really good game on Sunday. Can we go some other time?" Doug replied.

"Honey, I support you in your chosen activities. Every week you have chosen to watch about 12 hours of football. I love you and just want to spend one or two hours together so we can focus on each other."

Being a man who loves numbers, Doug saw the inequity of 12 hours of football tube time versus one or two hours of time alone together with his wife. Wanting to be a loving husband prompted Doug to change a little. He began spending more time with BJ on Sundays. Over the years football lost its strong appeal as their time together became more precious. BJ successfully convinced Doug a change was possible. It wasn't by whining or nagging, but by lovingly supporting his choices and at the same time gently reminding Doug he wasn't a bachelor any longer.

Anything that repeatedly takes us away from God's plan that the two shall become one (Genesis 2:24) could be labeled an obsession.

**The secret
of overcoming obsessive
behavior in marriage is. . .**
Knowing God's plan for your marriage and choosing to follow it.

Blinded by Anger

From Doug's Perspective

$\mathcal{B}$ased on the world's standards, Samson was a man's man. He was stronger than any other man and able to take any woman he wanted. He was proud of his abilities, but he was not a happy man. Samson had a serious problem with anger and rage. After losing a bet at his wedding reception, Samson was obligated to provide 30 sets of clothes to some of the Philistine guests. Enraged that he had lost the bet (his bride betrayed him in favor of her Philistine friends) he went out and killed 30 Philistines, stripped them, and delivered their clothes to the 30 wedding guests. Then, "burning with anger, he went up to his father's house" (Judges 14:19).

God's Word commanded Samson to honor his father and mother (Exodus 20:12). But when his parents pleaded with him not to marry the Philistine woman, Samson chose to do as he pleased and ignored them. When Samson lost the bet because of his wife's unfaithfulness, he flew into a rage, rather than reflecting on his actions and admitting to God and himself that he had sinned by not honoring his parents' wisdom. Anger had blinded him to the truth of his actions. That happened to me once. Would you believe twice? All right, it happened so many times I stopped counting.

Pride Sets Us Up for a Big Fall

What was it that caused Samson's anger? Sinful pride. We are allowed to take satisfaction in our accomplishments provided we recognize God's responsibility for those accomplishments. That is the good kind of pride (Galatians 6:4 and 1 Corinthians 1:26–31). However, when we take satisfaction in being better, superior, stronger than others, or refuse to acknowledge God for our abilities, that is sinful pride (Luke 18:9–14; Psalm 10:4).

Clearly God blessed Samson with extraordinary strength, ability, and a mission to lead Israel against the cruel dominion of the Philistines. Yet Samson did not acknowledge God for his abilities or accomplishments. His prideful attitude and behavior set him up for failure in his relationship with Delilah. Samson believed he could conquer anything.

Using persistence and guile, Delilah extracted the secret of Samson's strength—his uncut hair. She lulled him to sleep and had his head shaved. Yet even after his hair was gone (now *that* is something I can relate to), Samson believed he would be just as strong as before. Sinful pride. He mistakenly believed his strength came from his own doing. Samson didn't acknowledge God as the source of his strength. The Philistines subdued and enslaved Samson because of his downfall—pride.

Humility Defeats Anger

Pride often results in anger. In order to conquer the anger, one has to deal with the underlying issue of pride. This can be challenging because pride is like some cancers—hard to detect and equally as difficult to remove. Just ask Rick.

Rick had a lot going for him. He was married to a wonderful Christian woman, had three healthy children, enjoyed meaningful roles in church service, and had a rising career in the building industry. Life was good and Rick was a good husband and father. He was proud of his accomplishments, giving only lip service to God's provision in his life. He had not yet learned that "every good and perfect gift is from above, coming down from the Father of heavenly lights" (James 1:17).

Then Rick hit a bump in the road. The economy softened, his company dissolved, and he lost his job. Seven long years produced several new employers, all in different cities. The frequent moves were hard on his family, and his career was not advancing. Rick felt betrayed by God. He was filled with doubt, uncertainty, and moodiness. His family noticed the change as he became emotionally hurtful and uncommunicative. Anger became a regular part of his day as he used it to cover up his feelings of worthlessness, insignificance, and his distrust of God. Anger was masking his fear. Rick manipulated his wife and children in an attempt to control his out-of-control feelings. His self worth was dependent on his own efforts, but those efforts left him feeling inadequate and without significance in his life.

Then Rick experienced an epiphany. He realized he didn't trust God to provide for his family's needs or for the value and purpose in his life. His frustration over not being able to provide these things on his own terms and power caused his anger. It all stemmed from his prideful nature, believing he was in control.

Rick was determined to change. He humbled himself by admitting that he had wanted God's material gifts and blessings more than he wanted to know God personally. The truth was he couldn't provide for his family's needs by himself. His intelligence, talent, and even his ability to create income came from God. He apologized to his wife and children, asked them to forgive his past acts of anger and manipulation, and began a daily regimen of drawing closer to God for His goodness, not just for His gifts.

From Humility to Serenity

Now Rick seeks daily to be a man of humility and truth, trusting God for his livelihood and purpose in his life. Each day he strives to know Jesus better and has achieved a sense of serenity. He's not perfect, but his wife and children enjoy the husband and father he is becoming, his peaceful nature, his truthfulness about his shortcomings, and his willingness to give God the credit for all his abilities and accomplishments.

**The secret
of overcoming anger and rage is . . .**
Exchanging pride for humility and
God's serenity.

Feelings of Betrayal

From BJ's Perspective

*S*amson and Delilah's passionate love affair was doomed from the beginning. She was a Philistine woman who lived in a village just across the valley from Samson's house. He was to begin the deliverance of Israel from the rule of the Philistines. Their passions were their villains.

Samson and Delilah came together with hidden selfish motives and agendas. Seeking to satisfy momentary urges caused heartache to these famous lovers just like it did to me in the following story.

The Affair

Since fifth grade, Jodi and I had been best friends, growing up together in a small Midwestern town. We each married. Knowing she liked company while her Naval husband was out to sea, I dropped in unexpectedly at her house to spend a leisurely afternoon girl talking. The phone interrupted our conversation and Jodi answered it. Suddenly flustered, she quickly handed the phone to me, "It's your husband," she blurted out.

"What's up?" I asked into the phone.

"Stop messing around, Jodi." My husband said because he didn't recognize my voice. "This has to be quick, because BJ might walk in at any minute."

"What are you talking about?" I asked, laughing nervously.

"It's all set. She thinks I have to work overtime Saturday, so we'll meet same time, same place."

Slowly, I came to the realization that an illicit rendezvous was being planned. "Hey, do you know who you're talking to?" I asserted.

"See ya Saturday," he said in a provocative voice as he hung up.

Reeling from the shock of overhearing an affair being planned by my two closest friends, I handed the phone back to Jodi. "He thought he was talking to you about Saturday," I said as I gravitated toward the door in a trance, disbelieving what had just transpired.

"I'm so sorry. I was just so lonely," Jodi offered apologetically.

I had been bitten by the beast of betrayal through the selfish momentary needs and actions of my best friend and husband. That is, my former husband.

The Beast of Betrayal

Each ruler promised Delilah 28 pounds of silver for discovering the secret of Samson's supernatural strength. She greedily accepted the challenge.

"Tell me the secret of your great strength and how you can be tied up and subdued" (Judges 16:6), she implored of Samson. You've got to be kidding, Delilah! Why would Samson tell you how to subdue him? Maybe he thought it was some sort of sadistic lovers' game.

Their hot and heavy love affair must have added *Enquirer* type steamy gossip to the Valley of Sorek. Delilah repeated the same set-up four times—men hidden in her room whom she called to subdue Samson after their love-making. Wouldn't a smart person catch on a little quicker? Besides, I think I would be aware if people were hiding in my bedroom. Fool me once, shame on you. Fool me twice, shame on me. We're talking *four* times duplicating the same scene! That's the power of obsessions.

Because her persistent nagging was like a leaky faucet dripping on Samson's defenses, and his passion clouded his reasoning abilities, Samson eventually revealed the secret of his amazing strength. Can you believe he told her? Then they made love and Delilah put him to sleep on her lap. Once Samson fell asleep, she called a man to shave off the seven braids of his hair. Surprise, surprise.

Without his hair, his strength left him. What did Samson *think* would happen? Was he so assured of his strength that he assumed he was invincible? Hard to imagine until I remembered my own musings of immortality as a kid! How easy it is to judge.

Have You Been Betrayed?

Have you ever felt betrayed by someone you loved? It happens. I have felt the pangs of betrayal by loved ones eight times! Betrayal arouses many feelings. At different times I felt hurt, dumbfounded, exposed, deceived, taken advantage of, angered, retaliatory, tearful, unforgiving, disbelieving, incredulous, questioning, pained, horrible, weak, lesser than, sorrowful, and grief-stricken.

What does the Bible say? Forgive. Once? Twice? Seven times? Jesus said, "I tell you, not seven times, but seventy-seven times" (Matthew 18:22). Forgiveness is not for the sake of the betrayer or to let them off the hook. Forgiveness starts the process of healing for the betrayed.

On the other hand, what does it feel like to betray someone? I've been on that end, too. I sadly admitted I was living with a womanizing, abusive alcoholic who continually threatened my life. I packed my bags, loaded up half the furniture, our two sons, and their belongings, and we secretly moved out of our home while he was at work. I believed at that time divorce was the only solution to our unstable, godless marriage. I shudder to imagine the betrayal he felt upon returning to a nearly-empty house.

Being the perpetrator of betrayal, I rationalized my decision and felt justified, satisfied, vindicated, like a winner instead of a victim. But those feelings gave way to questioning, anxiety, and guilt. It still didn't seem right to deliberately scheme to hurt or destroy another. For twelve years I struggled to forgive and overcome regret. It is difficult to be on either side of betrayal.

Consequences of Betrayal
Because of Delilah's betrayal, Samson was subdued by the Philistines, and his eyes were gouged out. He was bound with bronze shackles, taken to the prison in Gaza, and subjected to hard labor. Horrendous repercussions for the betrayed.

I wonder how Delilah felt when her lover was painfully blinded and eventually killed. Was it worth the silver she gained? We have seen many times in biblical accounts that betrayal has not been worth the promised rewards. When Adam and Eve betrayed God, they were banished from the Garden of Eden. When Peter betrayed Jesus, Peter wept bitterly. After betraying Jesus, Judas threw away the reward money and committed suicide.

Feelings aroused by being the betrayer and betrayed are devastating. God offers a way to relieve those feelings: forgiveness.

Scriptural Steps to Forgiveness

Forgiveness starts in the head and transfers to the heart, not vice versa. Here are the steps that can lead us into forgiveness when it's hard to do on our own:

Repeat the Lord's Prayer. "For if you forgive men when they sin against you, your heavenly Father will also forgive you. But, if you do not forgive men their sins, your Father will not forgive your sins" (Matthew 6:14–15). God continually forgives. Our withholding forgiveness is like saying we know better than, or are wiser than God.

Realize that "not forgiving" gives Satan a foothold. "Do not give the devil a foothold" (Ephesians 4:27). "If there was anything to forgive—I have forgiven in the sight of Christ for your sake, in order that Satan might not outwit us. For we are not unaware of his schemes" (2 Corinthians 2:10–11). It's Satan's desire to separate us from God and from our spouse. Withholding forgiveness is akin to telling Satan, "Let me help you separate us."

Know an unforgiving spirit will result in bitterness. "See to it that no one misses the grace of God and that no bitter root grows up to cause trouble and defile many" (Hebrews 12:15). Our choice when we are wounded is becoming bitter or better.

Choose to forgive. Jesus said, "Father, forgive them, for they do not know what they are doing" (Luke 23:34). While Jesus hung on a cross in great physical and mental suffering, He chose to forgive those who had no idea what they had done. A spouse often doesn't understand how badly they have hurt us. Be like Jesus and forgive them anyway, in spite of their ignorance of what they have done.

Ask for God's help when forgiveness is difficult. "Do not be anxious about anything, but in everything, by prayer and petition, with thanksgiving, present your requests to God" (Philippians 4:6). Victory over the enemy is not won by ourselves alone.

Henry Ward Beecher warned us, "Saying I can forgive but I cannot forget, is only another way of saying, I will not forgive. Forgiveness ought to be like a canceled note— torn in two, and burned up, so that it never can be shown against one."

Forgiveness Prayer

Follow this sample prayer to help you forgive your spouse. Honestly express how your spouse hurt you. Pray *out loud* (but not necessarily in his/her presence):

"Lord, I forgive (*spouse*) for (*say what they did that hurt you*) even though it made me feel (*express the painful feelings and memories*)."

Conclude by praying: "Lord, I choose to forgive (*spouse*) and not hold this against (*spouse*) any longer. I thank you for setting me free from the bondage of my bitterness toward (*spouse*). I choose now to ask You to bless (*spouse*). In Jesus' name, I pray. Amen."

**The secret
of overcoming feelings
of betrayal is . . .**
Forgiveness.

Questions for Discussion and Action

1. Do you have an undesirable habit, addiction, or obsession that is separating you from God or your spouse? Where will you seek help?

2. Do you have a problem with anger or rage? How does it affect your marriage? What is causing your anger? What are you willing to do about it?

3. Have you ever felt betrayed in your marriage? Discuss the feelings it evoked in you with your spouse.

famous lovers

David and Bathsheba

2 Samuel 11–12

Caught Between Need and Greed
From BJ & Doug's Perspective

*W*ith God's help, David was a successful war hero who had victory over all his enemies and enjoyed the peace and prosperity it brought his kingdom. He was a wise ruler of a vast empire. David's strikingly handsome looks turned heads wherever he went, and his humble spirit attracted loyal followers. Best of all, David was chosen by God to be king because he was a man after God's own heart (1 Samuel 13:14). King David had more than "the good life"; he had the most generously endowed life of anyone up to that time in history.

David was a patient man and was not driven by greed. Before becoming king, he was a lowly shepherd, a harp player for King Saul, and a valuable servant in the king's army. As a military leader, he had two opportunities to take the throne from King Saul by force, but he refused. David knew killing Saul was contrary to God's Word, will, and plan. He waited for God's timing before taking the throne. David was not greedy. That is, until he saw Bathsheba.

In a moment of weakness, he sinned. When tempted,

he became rash, impulsive, and spontaneous. That behavior can get anyone, even a favored king, into deep weeds. What happened to cause such a drastic change?

Unbridled Desire

One night David could not sleep; he was restless, a dangerous place for a man to be. He was walking around on his roof. Guess what his wandering eye spied on a nearby roof? A woman bathing. A very beautiful woman. David impulsively decided he had to have her, even after he was told she was married to Uriah the Hittite. David wanted her so intensely he sent servants to get her, and he slept with her. But that's not the worst part of the story.

Why would David, a king who could call for any woman in his harem, a ruler who had the power and authority to take any unmarried woman in the kingdom as a wife, a man who was deeply devoted to God, throw his spotless record out the window with the bathwater for a one night stand with a stranger? Scripture is silent regarding his thoughts and reasoning. However, we do know David succumbed to temptation and sinned.

After he slept with Bathsheba, she became pregnant. David tried to cover up his impulsive adulterous act by bringing her husband Uriah home from battle in hopes he would sleep with Bathsheba. Then it would appear the pregnancy was Uriah's doing. But Uriah was a man of integrity. He didn't cooperate because honorable soldiers didn't sleep with their wives during wartime. When David's plan failed, he calculatingly had Uriah murdered so he could take Bathsheba as his wife. But even that's not the worst part of the story.

God sent Nathan the prophet to confront David with an incredibly convicting story about greed (2 Samuel 12:1–4).

David was slow to catch on until Nathan said, "You are the man!" Nathan described how David's sin impacted God. "This is what the LORD, the God of Israel, says: 'I anointed you king over Israel, and I delivered you from the hand of Saul. I gave your master's house to you, and your master's wives into your arms. I gave you the house of Israel and Judah. And if all this had been too little, I would have given you even more. Why did you despise the word of the Lord and do what is evil in His eyes?'" David broke God's heart. And that was the worst part of the story!

What's the Bottom Line?

If you think this story is about adultery, you're right. If you think this story is about murder, you're right. But if you think this story is only about adultery and murder, you're missing an important point. God wanted David to see that his adultery and murder were the by-products of the sin of greed.

David didn't wake up that fateful day planning on committing adultery and murder. His restlessness indicated he was not satisfied and wanted more. This is greed. When he spied Bathsheba, his greedy desire overpowered his righteous desire to obey God. One false step after another sucked him deeper into the quicksand of sin.

God has a big problem with greed, and He wanted David to realize it. God sent the prophet Nathan with a story that was not about adultery, not about murder, but about greed. It was about wanting something that belonged to someone else and taking something God provided to someone else. It was about wanting more, like Sue and Bill did in our next story.

Need or Greed Tested

After a whirlwind courtship of six months, Sue and Bill married, pulled up stakes in Boston, and purchased their dream house in San Diego. Eagerly they embarked on a new business venture: buying, fixing up, and reselling rental property. Then the real estate market took a nose-dive. Accrued business debt forced them to sell their beautiful home to pay the bills. They moved into the only rental property they still owned, a small, old two-story structure, located in a low-income neighborhood.

Not only was their new residence in deplorable condition, but they had to share it with three other families who had signed leases. Sue and Bill lived in the two small units on the top floor, while the bottom floor housed two immigrant families and a young couple. After overhearing their nightly activities, Sue and Bill surmised that the young couple earned their living selling drugs.

Sue struggled with depression because of the loss of their spacious home and the reality of their poverty. Both were disheartened and discouraged. It was a painful season of transition from their nice home in suburbia to living in an area where police sirens were a nightly occurrence and mortgage payments were a struggle.

Once the leases expired and their fellow occupants finally moved out, Bill put his construction expertise into use and restored the property. Sue had a gift for finding great "treasures" at various thrift shops and feathered their nest inexpensively but artistically. Together they transformed the once neglected, broken-down rental into a warm, funky, and charming home they grew to adore.

Bill and Sue persevered through their bleak circumstances and trials by praying and encouraging one another. God transformed their hearts to be content in all circumstances. They learned that material possessions did not bring lasting happiness. It wasn't as important as their love for one another. Sue and Bill came to realize that anywhere could be home as long as they kept their three-strand cord intact. They understand the difference between need and greed.

Distinguishing Between the Two

Nearly all of us are greedy from time to time. Greed is an insatiable sin that pulls us away from God like it did David. Try as we do to avoid being greedy, it is sometimes hard to distinguish between a need and greed. We use the following three questions to help determine whether our wants are *needs* or *greeds*:

- Will obtaining what I want break any of God's commandments?
- Will I be denying someone else what God provided for their need?
- Does this appear to be contrary to God's timing?
  If the answer to any of these questions is yes, then the desire is probably greed. David and Bathsheba's story can be used to show how these questions are helpful.

Will obtaining what I want break any of God's commandments?

Had David asked this question before summoning Bathsheba, he may have reconsidered his decision. At a minimum, David broke four of the Ten Commandments (Exodus 20:1–17). David put loving/seeking/lusting after women above loving/seeking God (idolatry). He coveted his neighbor's wife, committed adultery, and arranged for Uriah's murder to cover it up.

Will I be denying someone else what God provided for their need?

David was guilty of taking a wife God provided for Uriah. Bringing Bathsheba to the palace and lying with her was a sin against God and a sin against his neighbor. David could have looked at the situation from Uriah's perspective. That's what Nathan's story was all about. Then he would have realized his selfishness, covetous behavior, and greed.

Are we being greedy when we don't share our resources with the needy? The Scriptures are clear. God wants to bless you (Jeremiah 29:11), but the Scriptures are also clear that God wants to bless everyone, not just you (Matthew 5:45). Have you been doubly blessed? Then it may be time to share your good fortune with your neighbor.

Does this appear to be contrary to God's timing?

Adultery is never in God's plan or timing. Nor is greed, selfishness, or coveting. David knew God's heart and the importance of waiting for His timing. Seeking God's timing is crucial to avoiding greed. When David had the opportunity to take the throne from Saul by force, he refused because he realized it wasn't God's timing. Later, when Saul was killed by the enemies of Israel, David realized it was the right time to claim the throne.

Differentiating between need and greed is easier when looking at other couples' choices, but sometimes it is difficult in our own marriage. That's when we seek godly wisdom and counsel from trusted Christians. When we stop and honestly reflect on our choices and decisions, we give God an opportunity to speak to our hearts.

The Tie-Breaker

If, after answering these three questions and seeking wise counsel you still can't decide what to do, ask yourself, "Will this acquisition be used for God's purposes? Will it bring glory to God and build up His kingdom?" Here's how we applied these questions in our situation.

Newly married, we needed to buy a house, any house we could afford. In San Diego that is a huge challenge. We eventually located a pleasant little older residence within our budget and made an offer. It was accepted. During our attempt to get financing for the home, our mortgage broker asked us to stretch the truth (lie) on the mortgage application. We said no. He said we wouldn't be approved for the loan unless we did. We called our real estate agent and told her what our mortgage broker had said.

"Funny you called when you did," she said. "I just got off the phone with the sellers and they said their purchase of another home fell through and they really wanted to keep their house." We had a choice to make. Should we attempt to get other financing to buy this house, or cancel the purchase contract and let the sellers stay in their beloved home?

Referring to our need/greed questions was helpful to us:

• *Would our purchase of the home be contrary to God's commandments?* Lying on the application form would be contrary to God's commandments. However, we could have attempted to find other financing that did not require us to lie.

• *Would buying this house deny the needs of someone else?* The original owners decided they preferred staying in their home for practical, financial, and sentimental reasons. We could be denying them their need.

• *Was it contrary to God's timing?* The fact that we learned the sellers wanted to keep their house at just the same time we found out we could not get the loan was confirmation to us. Buying this house would have been contrary to God's best timing even though we wanted it. We canceled the purchase contract.

Consequence: about a month later, we toured a single story model home in a tract that offered new spacious homes. Careful calculations showed us that even with its larger house payment, we could afford it and still honor other financial commitments . . . barely . . . but it was doable.

We went to the sales office to make an offer to buy a *Plan One* house. The sales agent said, "The *Plan One* houses sold out the first day they were offered. People waited in line for over 36 hours to purchase that model!" Disappointed that we were about a month late, we thought maybe we were being too greedy wanting a new spacious home even though it seemed to fit our needs. Dejected, we turned to leave as the phone rang. The agent picked up the phone, talked, and hung up. Then he said, "That's amazing. We just had two escrows cancel. Both are *Plan Ones*. Which one would you like?"

Were we in the right place at the right time? Was it God's perfect timing?

We asked each other, "Will this house be used to build up God's kingdom?"

The *Plan One* floor plan had a large front room. Did we desire it for selfish reasons or did we envision holding church meetings? We had to examine our motives.

When the pastor who married us, Reverend Bob Morley, was a troubadour on tour in Russia, people asked about his living conditions. He told them he lived in a four-room house. They asked, "With how many families?"

We usually don't *need* bigger or better, but God is pleased when we use bigger for His benefit. We've since utilized the large living area for numerous Bible studies and church meetings.

Sometimes it is only with God's help that we can differentiate between need and greed. Knowledge of the Scriptures and staying connected with God through prayer will help save us from impulsive, sinful, or inappropriate choices and stay faithful to God's Word, will, and timing.

**The secret
of differentiating between
need and greed is . . .**
Seeking God's Word, will, and timing.

Busted for Lust

From Doug's Perspective

*I*n spite of all his great qualities, King David had a lustful eye. During his travels over the years, he accumulated seven wives and many concubines from different towns. After he became king, he inherited and took more wives and concubines. With a plethora of women to satisfy his every physical need, why did David want Bathsheba? Because lust knows no human boundaries, as we see in Jed's story.

Jed's Addiction

Jed's mother called to him as she walked out the front door "I'll be next door."

"Okay, Mom," Jed shouted back, as he returned his focus to laying out his baseball cards. He was hoping he had enough to create two full teams. Jed scowled. He was a few cards short. Then he remembered his dad had a baseball card collection somewhere. With the help of a step stool, his 8-year-old arms were just long enough to reach a box on the top shelf of his dad's closet. He hoped it contained the desired baseball cards.

Opening the box, Jed's eyes almost popped out of his head as he found himself staring at a naked woman in a magazine. His heart began to race as he flipped through the pages. From that day forward baseball cards never held the same allure as the provocative women splashed across the pages of the magazines his dad kept on the top closet shelf.

Jed grew into a handsome, intelligent man with a lucrative career and high profile job in television. However, lust had sucked him in at an early age and, like quicksand, had not let him go. The longer he dabbled in pornography, the deeper he sank. Even after marriage and children, he continued using this drug-of-choice. He loved his wife and children, but the sensual magnetic force of naked women in pictures held him in secret bondage.

Soon, even the raciest photos were not enough for Jed. He craved more. He began watching adult videos, and when he was away on business he sought out topless bars. Eventually, all of this erotic stimulation was not enough. He had become an addict looking for a bigger "fix." The extramarital affair lasted only a short time before his wife found out. She left him and took their children.

The emotional stress of being exposed and losing his family affected his job performance. He was demoted from the front lines where he liked to be. Jed, the once-bright rising star, was now fading as he sank deeper into the quicksand of addiction just like David had centuries before.

Consequences of David's Sin

The consequences of his sin eventually cost David the death of three sons. The first son that died was the baby born to Bathsheba. The baby was one week old. Then David's oldest son Amnon, who apparently learned from his father that lust was acceptable, began desiring to sleep with his half sister Tamar. Amnon tried to seduce Tamar, and when that failed, he raped her. Two years later, Tamar's brother Absalom killed Amnon in retaliation for his sister's rape.

After having killed Amnon, Absalom believed David would never allow him back into the family, so he mounted a revolt and attempted to forcefully take the throne from his father. David's forces subdued the revolt and Absalom was killed. All of this was prophesied to David through Nathan: "Now, therefore, the sword will never depart from your house, because you despised me and took the wife of Uriah the Hittite to be your own."

Sin cost David much more than he ever thought he would have to pay for his one night with Bathsheba. Fortunately, Jed's story has a different ending.

How Jed Broke the Addiction

Thirty-five years after he first found adult magazines in his father's closet, Jed stood in front of 80 men at a retreat to give his personal testimony. By this time, he had four years of abstinence from lusting. Graciously, his wife witnessed the change in him and agreed to reunite the family. After explaining in his testimony the pain he experienced, Jed outlined the steps he took toward restoring his integrity and purity:

He confessed the sin. "If we confess our sins, he is faithful and just and will forgive us our sins and purify us from all unrighteousness" (1 John 1:9). Confession is a necessary step.

Jed tried for years to stop lusting. He kept thinking if he

just used more will power he could stop. But the harder he tried to quit, the tighter the cords of sin enslaved him. Finally, with spirit broken and at rock bottom, he walked into a church. After that Sunday service, one of the elders noted his distress and comforted him. Later, as he sat in the pastor's office he revealed his story. The pastor said he had taken the first step—verbal confession. While Scripture requires confession to God, verbalizing our confession in the presence of a pastor or Christian counselor will provide a level of accountability.

He repented the sin. *Repent* means to turn completely away from, to have nothing to do with things that lead to lust anymore. The pastor urged Jed to repent.

The people of Israel, like our culture today, were overwhelmed with lust, adultery, iniquity, and debauchery in the time of Ezekiel the prophet. God spoke through him, saying "Repent! Turn away from all your offenses; then sin will not be your downfall. Rid yourselves of all the offenses you have committed, and get a new heart and a new spirit" (Ezekiel 18:30b–31a).

Repentance is not a half effort. It requires a complete and total commitment to be pure in heart. It means abandoning the sin to start a new life of purity.

It seemed like an impossible task, so Jed questioned the pastor, "How?"

The pastor said, "Temptation to sin can be strong, but God is always stronger." Then he quoted, "No temptation has seized you except what is common to man. And God is faithful; he will not let you to be tempted beyond what you can bear. But when you are tempted, he will also provide a way out so that you can stand up under it" (1 Corinthians 10:13). A pure heart will always look for God's escape plan when temptation comes.

He read the Bible daily. Morning is often recommended for Bible reading because it fortifies one for the temptations that will come during the day. Jed explained to the group of men that the Book of Proverbs is an excellent resource for those who are prone to lust. The book has 31 chapters, one for each day of the month. Jed reads one chapter per day, corresponding with that day's date. Proverbs 5, 6, and 7 were particularly helpful to him.

He prayed daily. Morning prayers prepare your heart and mind for the day's temptations. Jesus warned, "Pray that you will not fall into temptation" (Luke 22:40).

Some men get up to pray before anyone else in their house is awake. Other men pray in their cars on the way to work. When you choose this option, don't bow your head too long! One friend of mine arrives at work 15 minutes early each day so he can pray in his parked car before he faces the inevitable temptations brought on by women who dress provocatively at work.

He had an accountability partner. This was a must for Jed. United we stand, divided we fall. No one can stand up to the attacks of the enemy singularly. In order to keep on track, pastors recommend having a person, church group, or group who would be willing to hold you accountable. "As iron sharpens iron, so one man sharpens another" (Proverbs 27:17). With God, a trusted accountability partner, and our commitment, we have a three-strand cord of resistance to sin that cannot be easily broken (Ecclesiastes 4:12).

He didn't go back there. If your problem is the computer or Internet, get an effective filter, or change your email address, or have a friend or your spouse check your computer to hold you accountable. A pastor friend doesn't even go on the Internet until his secretary sets it up. If it's a dangerous place to be like the beach, surfing channels on TV, or R-rated movies, don't let temptation into your eyesight.

He focused his thoughts and attention on his wife. Dwell on your wife's best qualities. Pay attention to what is happening in her life, and find a way to help her. Whenever temptation leads you astray, whether it is in your dreams, during the act of making love, or at the beach, don't allow your mind to go there or even wander a little.

Clean Sweep

Jed concluded his testimony with one final thought. "Suppose you had a carpet which was full of dirty spots, but you cleaned the carpet and applied an anti-spotting agent so that it could no longer get spots. In time, you would forget about the spots that were on your carpet.

"But suppose you cleaned the carpet and left just one small spot. Every time you looked at the nearly clean carpet your eye would be drawn to look at the dirty spot. It is like that with lust. If you permit yourself just one pleasure, just one photo, just one video, your life will continually be drawn to it. The dark spots of your life must be completely removed, never to be seen again."

Confession, repentance, Bible reading, daily prayer, accountability, and commitment to focusing thoughts solely on his wife worked for Jed and many others. It can work for you, too, when you make that choice. Jesus is asking you the same question He asked the sick man laying beside the pool: "Do you want to get well?" (John 5:6).

When Loneliness Strikes

From BJ's Perspective

I tried to analyze Bathsheba's part in the story of these famous lovers. Unfortunately, we know little about her feelings and intentions once she became involved with King David. Was she:

- Being obedient and submissive, or did she try to resist David?
- Was Bathsheba filled with loneliness, passion, and lustful thoughts? Or was she a victim to an insistent, impulsive king?
- Was she a scheming seductress poised for entrapment? Or was the innocent wife going about her business in the privacy of her own home?

Her motives are unknown. But I wanted to learn from her experience, and I have many thoughts and unanswered questions.

I understand:	I don't understand:
• Bathsheba was bathing, and David could see her.	• Why could people see her bathing?
• She was exceptionally beautiful.	• How could David tell from a distance?
• Her husband was away.	• Was she lonely?
• David sent more than one person to get her.	• Why? Wouldn't she go willingly?
• David wanted her, so he had his way with her.	• Did she resist? Was it actually rape?
• She conceived, and sent a note that she was pregnant.	• How did she feel about the pregnancy?
• Uriah was brought home.	• Did Bathsheba know David's plan?
• She became a widow.	• Was she aware David had Uriah murdered?
• David married her.	• Did she feel guilt /pride/ shame?
• She became one of David's many women.	• Which was better—being poor and an only wife, or being wealthy and one of many wives?
• She bore the king a son who died days later.	• Did she blame God, David, Satan, or herself?
• They conceived Solomon, who was in the lineage of Jesus.	• God still uses imperfect people who make major mistakes.

Comparison

In Biblical times, women were second-rate citizens. They were commodities. All of the king's people were subject to his requests. David's passionate impulses ruled. He took what was off limits in God's eyes. Sounds like rape to me. Was Bathsheba a seductress or a victim? A little of both? Who was at fault? The bottom line is that rape is always the fault of the perpetrator.

Is it possible that Bathsheba faced the same issue that so many married women face today? *Loneliness.* Mother Teresa, in her book *The Simple Path*, said it's the number one problem in the United States. Temptation lurks at the doors of lonely wives when husbands are away on business trips, away at sea or war, ill, or emotionally unavailable. Whatever the case for loneliness, we can make choices we won't regret in the morning. We need to guard our hearts and minds in Christ Jesus. Here are some of the many ways to do that.

Fellowship with God on a daily basis. God wants to be the center of our thoughts and attention. He wants to be our best friend and the love of our lives, someone we can pour our hearts out to. He is always there to listen and to bring comfort and peace, even in the loneliest times. Praying keeps the communication lines open with God. It helps us appreciate the goodness, the patience, and the discipline of God.

Keep company with other Christian women who can hold you accountable. The best way to avoid temptation and sin is to *hang out* with other like-minded women who are seeking to keep their hearts pure.

When I first moved to San Diego I was a lonely single parent. In seeking adult conversation and companionship, I sought out bars that were frequented by singles. I quickly discovered many lonely people were looking for a different way of relieving loneliness! It wasn't only the smoke-filled atmosphere that left me feeling estranged, disillusioned, and lonelier than before. Smoke screens, bar attendees, and one-night-stands were not the solutions to my plight.

Start a journal of love letters to your husband or to Jesus. Writing thoughts and feelings on paper helps to alleviate loneliness. You don't have to ever show anyone the letters or mail them. We may think of other men because 50% of the people in the world are males, but the wise woman doesn't have to entertain impure thoughts or fantasies of them. Writing to or about one's husband keeps our thoughts pure and focused.

Read books on what to do when you are lonely. Some helpful ones I have found are *When Women Walk Alone*, by Cindi McMenamin; *Woman Of Influence* by Pam Farrel; *Abiding In Christ* by Cynthia Heald; and *Experiencing God* by Henry Blackaby and Claude King. Or you can visit your local or church's library and ask for appropriate reading materials. Reading steamy novels may only add to your difficulties.

Volunteer to work with others who are lonely. Widowers, shut-ins, convalescent home residents, military wives, and support groups are good places to reach out to others instead of focusing on self.

When I was bedridden for five months because of three surgeries, it got lonely. I was plagued by a "not spot" (a place where joy is not). Crying out to God in prayer, I was inspired to reach out to others who also were lonely. I could make phone calls, write postcards, or send letters. It helped me stop thinking only about my pain, my plight, and my pitiful problems. It transported me from the pit of depression onto the mountaintop of thinking about and helping others.

Join special interest groups. If you have hobbies, look for others who share your interests. Stay away from groups or places that you know will be tempting for you to seek companionship, sympathy, or attention from the opposite sex. Seek activities that are fulfilling to you and to connect with others who enjoy the same.

Get involved with a Bible Study or church group. If your church doesn't offer women's Bible studies, other churches in your area probably do. Let your fingers do the searching. Offer your home for a study, or teach a women's Bible Study yourself. Perhaps you could start a study in your neighborhood.

Don't set yourself up for failure or temptation. As Mom put it, "Don't put it in your shopping cart if you know you shouldn't have it." Stay away from one-on-one meetings with the opposite sex. One pastor friend has a rule to never ride alone in a vehicle with the opposite sex. Another has a window in the office door so all meetings are in full public view. One pastor doesn't want to be surprised by anything on the Internet or in his email, so he doesn't use it.

I found out the hard way that going to bars and places where temptation lurks is asking for trouble that will probably find me. If someplace is tempting for you, don't even go there.

Volunteer in your community or church. A safe way to get out of self-thinking is by other-thinking. Volunteering by reaching out to assist other causes or needs helps alleviate loneliness.

**The secret
of dealing with loneliness is . . .**
getting involved in appropriate activities,
reaching out to other lonely people, and
trusting in God!

Questions for Discussion and Action

1. What area of greed do you struggle with the most? What can you do as a couple to conquer greed in your marriage?

2. How do you deal with lustful thoughts and temptations? Which of the ideas in this chapter will you incorporate into your life?

3. How do you deal with feelings of loneliness in your life or marriage? What new choices will you commit to making?

famous lovers

*King Xerxes
and Esther*

Esther 1–8

Recognizing Defining Moments
From BJ & Doug's Perspective

The story of Esther and King Xerxes (also known as Ahasuerus) is about famous lovers who made wise choices during defining moments. Defining moments present us with opportunities to redefine who we are, the character we want to build, and how we will be remembered.

King Xerxes was a powerful ruler whose kingdom stretched from modern-day India to Egypt. He gave a party for friends and noblemen that lasted six months. Is this a Guinness world record? He asked his wife, Queen Vashti, to come to the party and dance for his friends, but she refused. His anger burned. It was a defining moment for the king. Based on lame advice and poor judgment, he decided to divorce her.

Esther was a beautiful, shy young woman. She pleased the king and was chosen to become his new queen. Esther was too timid to reveal her Jewish identity at that time. Later it would play a major part in a life-saving defining moment.

The Rest of Their Story

Haman was King Xerxes' friend, top aide, advisor, and business manager. He was a self-centered, egotistical, and diabolical man. Haman hated Jews and wanted them annihilated. Using deception, he induced King Xerxes to issue an irrevocable decree that would be carried out 11 months later.

Queen Esther's cousin Mordecai told her of the decree to "destroy, kill and annihilate all the Jews" (Esther 3:13). He urged her to intercede with the king on behalf of all Jews. Esther was reluctant to help because the law stated that anyone who approached the king without being summoned would be put to death, unless the king made an exception by raising his gold scepter.

Mordecai was a wise man. He informed Esther that God would rescue the Jews one way or another, but added, "Who knows but that you have come to royal position for such a time as this?" Esther faced a defining moment in her life. Would she continue to be the shy, dutiful, submissive queen, or would she take this opportunity to be bold for God and her people?

Esther risked all and approached the king. The king raised his gold scepter and invited her to speak. She asked the king to bring Haman and come to a dinner she would prepare for them. He agreed and that night the king and Haman dined with Esther. For the second time, Xerxes asked Esther what she wanted. Again she asked him to come to dinner tomorrow night with Haman. Her newly developing courage enabled her to refuse to directly answer the king twice, as she waited for the right moment.

After the men had eaten and drunk their fill, she appealed to the king, in a very diplomatic way, to save the life of every Jew, including her own. She also exposed Haman as the vile enemy who concocted the plan to annihilate the Jews.

Now King Xerxes faced a defining moment. Would he side with his close friend or would he be a loyal and faithful husband? Xerxes made an immediate decision to support his wife. He ordered Haman executed and then issued a decree allowing the Jews to protect themselves. The Jews were saved because Esther and King Xerxes made God-honoring choices when faced with defining moments.

Transformation

King Xerxes and Esther, before their defining moments, could be described as king and queen, dominant and subservient, with limited communication. The remainder of their lives could have been lived like this, but God had a different plan for their marriage. A metamorphosis occurred in Esther, King Xerxes, and their marriage because of their choices in these two defining moments.

Before	After
Esther	
Only outer beauty seen	Inner character developed
Naive	Wise beyond her years
Timid	Courageous
King Xerxes	
Party animal	Loving husband
Views wife as sex object	Has concern for wife's views

Before	After
Their Marriage	
Superficial	Meaningful union
Dominant / subservient	Husband / helpmate
Limited communication	Close involvement

Our Defining Moment

After two years of marriage, Doug confessed he had not stopped drinking as he had promised before we were married. BJ felt betrayed. Having been married previously to an abusive alcoholic, Doug's confession depressed and frightened her. She wanted to divorce. Doug, however, appealed for her to wait; he would get the necessary help to stop drinking.

Our marriage faced a defining moment. We knew God hated divorce (Malachi 2:16). BJ suffered with regret for twelve years after breaking her wedding covenant to God when she divorced her first husband. How could she stay in this marriage with no guarantee things would be different from the first? Could she trust God for deliverance from the terrible dynamics created by alcoholism?

After heartfelt prayer and much discussion, we recommitted to persevering in our marriage. We chose a plan of action that included daily prayer, daily Bible reading, and daily time for confession of sins to each other. Through God's grace and our faithfulness to the plan, we began the journey of rebuilding our broken marriage and have been grateful for Doug's sobriety since 1987.

Your Defining Moment

What one word or phrase best describes your marriage? Is your relationship known for love, devotion, commitment, tension, emotional distance, or separate paths? We all have some area of our marriage we'd like to change or improve—and we're talking about what each can personally do to improve (not what I want my spouse to do differently).

Maybe this is a defining moment for you. You can make a God-honoring decision to become all that God wants you to be in your relationship by working on a character weakness. "I can do everything through him [Christ] who gives me strength" (Philippians 4:13). There are four steps that will help you implement change and improvement:

1. Decide on one area that needs improvement. It may be listening more, being open to what I can learn from my spouse, helping out around the house, calendaring time alone together, praying together daily, etc. Tackling one thing at a time will elevate your chances of success and help you focus.

2. Commit it to writing. Be specific. Example: "I will be a better listener by stopping what I'm doing and looking my spouse in the eye when she wants to talk to me." Perhaps you'd like to grow spiritually. You could write, "I will get up 15 minutes earlier each morning to read my Bible and pray." By writing down your intention and posting it in a prominent place, like on a bathroom mirror, computer, or in the car, you will see it often. The more you read it and take it into your heart, the easier it will be to keep on track.

3. Ask for accountability. Ask someone (preferably your spouse) to help you. Two is better than one, and a three-strand cord is not easily broken (Ecclesiastes 4:12). Be specific in asking for what you need, such as, "Would you remind me to look at you when you speak?" Or, "Could you set the alarm clock 15 minutes earlier and push me out of bed when it goes off?" It is advisable to let your accountability partner know what would not work also— tone of voice, volume, nagging, etc. Ask Jesus for help, too, in remembering your commitment. Try this plan for a minimum of 30 days until it becomes a habit. (More about accountability partners in chapter nine.)

When we get off track or forget, we love it when the other *gently* reminds us of our chosen intention. For instance, "I love it when you look me in the eyes while I'm talking. I feel heard." This is positive affirmation, rather than, "You never listen. You promised you would and I already had to remind you three times this week."

4. Evaluate. Regularly evaluate yourself. Also, ask your accountability partner, "How am I doing?" It helps to see progress and reminds us if we get sidetracked. This necessary review needs to be conducted at a set time daily or weekly, or it won't happen.

Each step in this four-part plan is essential for success. Try it, you'll like it—'cause it works! While you can have significant short-term improvement by using just one, two, or three of the steps, you'll have more long-term success with the plan if you use all four steps together. And you want your marriage to be good for the long haul! The following Action Plan Chart visibly shows the success rates of implementing two, three, or four steps. It looks like this:

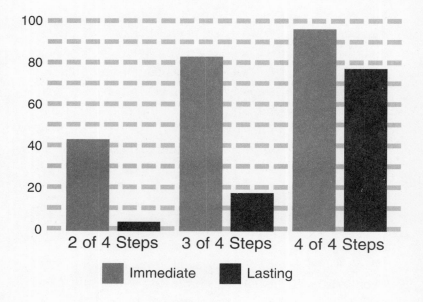

Percentages of Immediate Improvement and Lasting Improvement

To achieve the highest success rate of change and behavior modification, implement all four steps of this Action Plan. For longest lasting improvement, the odds are substantially in your favor when you:
1. Choose one thing at a time to work on.
2. Write out a specific plan.
3. Ask for accountability.
4. Evaluate often.

> **The secret
> to refining character is . . .**
> Choosing wisely in defining moments and
> implementing an action plan for
> improvement.

Spending Time Together

From Doug's Perspective

Before he met Esther, King Xerxes was married to Queen Vashti. After a long party for the men (reading between the lines: lots of alcohol, impaired reasoning, no time for his wife), the King sent an *order* to Queen Vashti to make an appearance at the party, probably so that the King could impress his guests with her beauty. Not a wise move. The queen refused to go, and even refused to give a reason why she would not attend (reading between the lines: "How dare you order me to come to your stag party. For that you get the silent treatment.") This angered the king, and after consulting his closest friends, he decided to divorce Vashti.

What caused the divorce of this regal couple? Was it her refusal to attend the party, the fact she didn't give an explanation, or because he was disgraced? One thing is sure, their divorce resulted from the lack of direct, quality conversation. Could this situation occur today? Ha! The question is not *if* there will be a lack of communication in our marriage, but what to do *when* it happens. So what will we do?

A Plan to Resolve Tough Issues

King Xerxes had another chance to learn the art of effective communication when he married Queen Esther. At first, he called for her often—after all, he chose her because she pleased him most. However, as time went on he called for her less often. When Esther made the courageous decision to approach the king, he had not called for her in a month (Esther 4:11)

Then King Xerxes made a decision that threatened his beloved Esther's life. He ordered the annihilation of all the Jews. He didn't realize Esther was a Jew. When Esther was told about the king's decree, she formulated a plan. Esther's plan was to reconnect with her husband through quantity and quality time together. Here's how the three-step plan worked.

Agree on a time to meet. First, Esther boldly came before Xerxes and asked that he attend a special dinner she was preparing for him. How would he react? In marriage sometimes it is difficult to take the first step in attempting to reopen communication. Too often we assume the other is upset and unwilling to communicate, only to find they are eager to resolve some difficult issue. Esther was rewarded for her courage because Xerxes agreed to hear her out during their dinner meeting.

Allow time to just "be" together. Second, Esther's plan was to spend a *quantity* of time with the king. Notice that Esther did not immediately appeal to Xerxes to save the Jews. First she spent an enjoyable evening with him to re-establish intimacy in their relationship, to get reacquainted, and to remember the reasons they married in the first place. It appears Xerxes was perfectly willing to discuss the matter right away, but Esther knew that communication is enhanced after a couple has spent a *quantity* of time together.

After a loving connection is reestablished, discuss the important issue. Third, Esther moved ahead to serious *quality* time together. Esther's methodology was successful. After two full nights of eating, drinking, and conversation, Esther made her appeal to save the Jews. Xerxes was ready to listen.

Quality Conversation Is Talking and Listening

It was a challenge communicating with Dennis. Actually, it wasn't talking to Dennis that was difficult; it was waiting for his response. I was a fast talker and a slow listener. He was the opposite. I instinctively wanted to fill the long silent pauses in our conversations with words. One day I chose to have patience and just listen. At first Dennis offered small bits of disjointed talk. Still, I talked little and listened intently. To my amazement, after what seemed like five minutes of awkward communication, he began sharing about his life, dreams, the meaning of life, and what he wanted to accomplish more than anything else in the world. I was amazed at the depth of his thinking, and that he trusted me enough to share such intimate thoughts.

How sad it is to see marriage partners not listen to

each other. We have witnessed numerous couples sabotage communications because one does all the talking. We are tempted to shout to the talkative one, "Just listen!"

Stephen, a very quiet man, married Leslie, a very talkative woman. Leslie's criticism was that Stephen never communicated with her about important issues. Stephen's main complaint was that Leslie spoke nonstop at 400 to 600 words per minute with gusts upward of 800 wpm. It was hard to figure out how she managed to breathe between sentences.

We were visiting their home, listening to Leslie's never ending flood of words. Okay, we admit we were only half listening as we were trying to filter out the repetitions. Suddenly, there was an unexpected lull in the conversation, as if we were suddenly in the eye of a hurricane. I looked at Stephen to see if he would seize this opportunity to speak. Just as I sensed he was ready, *wham*, the hurricane returned and we were overpowered by Leslie's diatribe again. I learned a valuable lesson that day. When I think I need to fill the silence with words, I can open communication lines by *just listening*.

There are many ways to spend quality and quantity time together conversing and listening. Take for instance, the couple in our next story.

Meet Jon and Cindi

Jon extended the opened invitation for his high school reunion to Cindi. She did *not* want to go. He was excited about reliving a wonderful time in his life. She was not. The images of the previous reunion flashed in her mind: strangers drinking too much, bragging about what they thought would impress others, making empty promises never intended to be kept.

Reunions were not Cindi's idea of fun. She'd rather relax in a hot bath and renew her frazzled soul. She didn't think she would have the strength to step into a competitive reunion arena that evening. People would be scrutinizing her dress, hair, face, and jewelry and pumping her husband for information about what line of work he was in, how much money he made, or what kind of car he drove.

Cindi sympathized with Queen Vashti. Perhaps *she* was tired the night King Xerxes summoned her to the party. Perhaps the queen didn't want to be on display. Perhaps Queen Vashti needed a soak in a hot bath, too.

The tired wife tried to convince her husband to go without her. Jon listened to the excuses and then quietly stated, "But I want to go with my pretty wife." Cindi looked in the mirror and sighed. She wasn't feeling very pretty that day, but she acquiesced.

As they walked into the reunion, the melody played by the live band took them back in time to the late '70s. Jon reveled in telling his treasured high school memories as Cindi listened to stories she hadn't heard before. Classmates stopped by their table to reminisce.

Jon requested the last dance from Cindi, and they walked hand-in-hand to the dance floor. He slipped his arm through hers and playfully spun her around. It turned out to be a wonderfully romantic evening. Cindi thought how different this night could have been. Her heart smiled with the realization Jon had chosen her to share a dance, an evening, a lifetime. That night Cindi understood the difference between an attitude of *having* to spend time with her husband (a duty) . . . or *getting* to be with him (a privilege).

Who Are You Spending Time With?

From Jon's point of view, the time spent with Cindi at the reunion was *quality* time. She didn't expect to have quality time with him, but settled for a *quantity* of time together. Their marriage was rewarded because of their *quantity* and *quality* (Double "Q") time spent together.

Some people think that wedging brief periods of quality time with a spouse between work, kids, and other commitments is sufficient to insure a good marriage. That is misleading. If your desire is to build the strongest marriage possible, it is advisable to invest large blocks of time with your spouse to insure the time you do spend is of high value and meaningful.

Jim and Pam are married with five children. They designate a couple of hours each week to be alone together. To them, this is a large block of time, considering they both work outside the house and both participate in activities with their children. Pam said that invariably the first hour of their time alone together is spent disagreeing over issues with work, school, children, schedules, priorities, money, etc. Yet, after getting past all the details of marriage and childrearing, they are able to relax and just enjoy each other. The point is that time alone to discuss important issues is necessary—quality time—but unless we extend the time, too—quantity time—we will miss the intimate time we need together.

In Conclusion

Our spouse doesn't have an intimacy switch which can be turned on and off at our preference. Intimacy doesn't exist because we have one quality conversation. It happens when we choose to spend quantity and quality time together, communicating and listening to each other.

When we invest time and energy into developing our marital relationship, intimacy is the dividend. Our love for each other grows in proportion to the time and energy we invest.

**The secret
of building intimacy is . . .**
Spending quantity and quality
time together.

Courage in the Face of Adversity

From BJ's Perspective

*E*sther's cousin Mordecai raised her in the Jewish tradition to be a submissive and obedient female. These characteristics endeared her to others. From orphan to harem girl to queen, Esther was a gentle soul who accepted her circumstances without complaint. She acquiesced to people and circumstances, but not to fear. Esther's story demonstrates how we can be one of God's faithful servants whatever the season, whatever our station of life, whatever our apprehension.

Courage is a state or quality of mind or spirit that enables us to be steadfast in meeting danger or adversity with bravery. Jill Briscoe articulated at the Anne Graham Lotz Conference in San Diego, "Courage is doing it frightened." Anne said, "Courage is standing up on the inside." Even though she was trembling, Esther went before the king. How did she overcome her fear? By taking action in spite of fear. Esther had a choice: do nothing and risk her life if Haman found out she was a Jew, or muster up the courage to approach the throne and risk death. Quite a choice!

After reading about Esther, my definition of courage is "being afraid and doing it anyway." It doesn't have to be a fearful life and death situation like Esther's to help us rise to the occasion as seen in the following story.

Being Afraid and Doing It Anyway

Doug and I honeymooned in Hawaii on the island of Maui in January of 1986. Friends told us about a must-see attraction, the Seven Sacred Pools. Being a professional photographer, I salivated at their description of the awesome beauty of seven natural pools, one overflowing to the other to form a breathtaking, cascading waterfall. I envisioned a photo capturing the scene, framed and hanging on the wall of our apartment.

There was a catch. It was located at the end of a long and winding three-hour trek over a treacherous, potholed road, and I was prone to severe motion sickness. Would a Kodak moment be worth *hours* of suffering and the possible embarrassment of regurgitating in front of my new husband? We were assured the reward would outweigh my apprehension of getting there.

I encountered a defining moment when we faced "the Road to Hana." Would I let fear rule? Hesitantly, I decided to go for it. After three hours of sickening jostling over the jarring road, we arrived at our destination. There had been an unexpected drought that year, and the sight we saw at the end of the road to Hana was best described as "The Seven Unsacred Small Mud Puddles!"

Even though I felt disappointed and discouraged, the trip was not a total loss. I learned I could victoriously walk through my fear of being motion sick that had so often held me back from fun adventures. Now I could fearlessly face the road *back* from Hana!

Courage Without Reward

Courage does not always provide material rewards. William Tyndale of England was a religious reformer in the sixteenth century. He believed God wanted everyone to have the opportunity to read the Bible in their own native language. However, King Henry VIII did not approve his request to translate the Bible from Latin to English. Tyndale was faced with a defining moment and monumental decision. Translate the Bible into English and expose himself to the wrath of the king and other powerful religious leaders, or abandon the project.

In 1525 he translated the New Testament into English and it was secretly made available to the public. Tyndale continued his translation and duplication of the entire Bible until he was arrested, imprisoned for over a year, then burned at the stake for heresy. Because of his courage in the face of adversity, opinions were eventually changed in England. As the English Reformation progressed after Tyndale's death, more translations were made of the Bible into English, the prime example of which is the King James Version of the Bible. (You can read about William Tyndale in chapter twelve of *Foxe's Book of Martyrs*.)

Courage may or may not produce worldly reward, but it can produce an inward satisfaction of knowing we have done God's will and that we will not be ruled by fear.

Courage in Esther's Adversity

Torn by her fear and her devotion to her Jewish heritage, Queen Esther courageously chose to approach the king for the express purpose of asking pardon for the Jews.

Before approaching King Xerxes, Esther asked the Jews in Susa, where the royal palace was and where Mordecai lived, to fast for three days while she herself fasted. Through the acts of fasting and prayer, Esther drew closer to God's will and plan for her life and was fortified by God's power when the time came to approach Xerxes. What a powerful witness.

King Xerxes was intrigued by Queen Esther's courage. Instead of asking outright for a pardon for the Jewish people, Esther extended dinner invitations, two nights in a row. Did she lose her nerve in this frightening situation or was it part of God's plan to invite them to dinner twice? I'd like to think it was God's plan she was faithfully following.

The king's sympathies leaned toward granting Esther anything she wanted, up to half his kingdom. I imagine the king was really getting curious by now about what was on Esther's mind. When asked once again to name her petition, Esther answered, "If I have found favor with you, O king, and if it pleases your majesty, grant me my life—this is my petition. And spare my people—this is my request. For I and my people have been sold for destruction and slaughter and annihilation" (Esther 7:3–4).

"Esther again pleaded with the king, falling at his feet and weeping. She begged him to put an end to the evil plan of Haman the Agagite, which he had devised against the Jews" (Esther 8:3). King Xerxes's heart was softened by Esther's respectful approach and he granted her wish.

Courage Builds Intimacy

The stakes aren't often as high in our marriages, but the courage to communicate what is on our mind and heart can build deeper respect and intimacy. Do we keep quiet because we are afraid of the way our spouse will react? Does fear of reprisal cause us to be weak in the knees? Fear paralyzes, while courage allows us to advance in spite of the fear.

In our marriage, whether it is in difficult communication situations, reconciliation, or in intimacy, I have been blocked by fear in taking the initiative to approach Doug with my requests. It may be fear of rejection or the fear of Doug *wanting* me to approach him more! But my shy self grew when I chose to change my ways. I have seen how it softens Doug's heart and how he enjoys my sharing what is on my heart. Our marriage has grown and improved because I chose to change. King Xerxes and Queen Esther developed a deeper relationship after making courageous choices in spite of their feelings of vulnerability.

**The secret
of overcoming fear is . . .**
Advancing in spite
of being afraid.

Questions for Discussion and Action

1. What fear do you face in your marriage? With God's help can you discuss it with your spouse?

2. What will you do to spend more quantity and quality time with your spouse?

3. In what area of your character do you want to grow? What steps will you use to succeed?

*Joseph
and Mary*

Matthew 1:18–25

Luke 1:26–38

The Chosen

From BJ & Doug's Perspective

After the angels told Mary and Joseph they were chosen by God to parent His one and only son, did they ask "Why us"? Did they recognize that their assignment from God was challenging, dangerous at times, and required them to stretch in their faith? So why would anyone want to work for God? Because every job well done, no matter how big or how small, comes with God's special blessing. For Mary and Joseph, that blessing was getting to know Jesus in the flesh, to touch Him, to hold Him, to hug Him, and to watch Him grow into becoming the Savior of the world.

Why did God choose ordinary people like Mary and Joseph? Why would He choose ordinary people like you, like us, for His special assignments? The world chooses according to looks, smarts, wealth, connections, or abilities. God chooses for other reasons. "Man looks at the outward appearance, but the LORD looks at the heart" (1 Samuel 16:7). What is it that God looks for in our hearts? What essential qualities did God see in Mary and Joseph's hearts? We believe these famous lovers were chosen because they were morally pure, because they extended grace and mercy to other people, and because they had servant hearts.

Desiring Moral Purity

Mary was a woman of moral purity. "God sent the angel Gabriel to Nazareth, a town in Galilee, to a virgin pledged to be married to a man named Joseph, a descendant of David. The virgin's name was Mary" (Luke 1:26–27). After the angel told Mary "You will be with child and give birth to a son," she questioned how this would happen. She knew God would not approve of her having sexual relations with Joseph before marriage. She was told the Holy Spirit would come upon her. In spite of the shame and disgrace pre-marital pregnancy brought in those days, Mary was faithful to God. "'I am the Lord's servant,' Mary answered. 'May it be to me as you have said'" (Luke 1:38).

Joseph was a man of moral purity. He had no sexual relations with his betrothed before marriage. Even after Joseph wed Mary, he was keenly aware of the need for moral integrity.

On our wedding night, I (Doug) admit I had only one thing in mind once we got to the hotel room. But Joseph refrained until after the birth of Jesus. We believe he abstained from sex with Mary so there would be no question that the baby Jesus was from His heavenly Father rather than His earthly father.

Theirs must have been a unique honeymoon:

"Joseph, would you like to watch the sunset together, or take a walk?"

"No, I think I'll take another dip in the lake. The frigid waters will be a blessing."

God specially blessed Mary and Joseph because of

their moral purity. Moral purity is a responsibility for those who want to experience God's special blessings.

The Chosen Extend Grace and Mercy

Grace is receiving a blessing you don't deserve. Mercy is not receiving punishment you do deserve. God is the author of grace and mercy. Through faith in Jesus Christ, we do not die, as we deserve, for our sins. We receive the blessing of eternal life, which we don't deserve and cannot earn. As recipients of grace and mercy, we are called to reflect God's image and to extend grace and mercy to others.

Two thousand years ago marriages were arranged by families. Mary and Joseph were probably chosen for each other by their parents and then introduced to the whole village as betrothed. Once the announcement was made, relatives orchestrated the wedding ceremony and celebration. Engagements were covenants as sacred as marriage itself and lasted as long as a year. It was a time for planning and preparation.

During the engagement, Mary was told by an angel she would become pregnant by the Holy Spirit. How did she explain the unexplainable to Joseph? We wonder if the conversation went something like this:

"Joseph, I don't know how to tell you this but, . . . I'm pregnant."

"You can't be serious."

"I am very serious."

"How can this be?"

"The Holy Spirit came upon me."

"The Holy Spirit came upon you and . . . what?"

"And I'm pregnant."

"Riiiiight!!"

Admitting to being *with child* was the most shocking announcement Mary could have delivered to Joseph. He undoubtedly felt a severe sting, as if slapped on the face, by her disclosure. He knew that he was not the father of the child, and must have feared the worst—that she had been unfaithful to him. Unfaithful wives could be put away, exiled or possibly stoned to death.

Announcing to the townsfolk that his intended young bride-to-be was no longer pure and innocent was an option for Joseph. Retribution would have been justified for such an apparent betrayal. But Joseph was compassionate and did not want to expose her to public disgrace. In spite of his humiliation, Joseph "had in mind to divorce her quietly" (Matthew 1:19). He was not only a godly man of high moral purity, but a man of grace and mercy. He refused to retaliate against Mary for what appeared to be her moral failure.

Then Joseph was visited by an angel who verified the authenticity of Mary's explanation. Joseph's decision to continue with the marriage plans was an act of grace, obedience, and faith. His heart allowed him to make the right choice when faced with a tough moral dilemma.

What a great lesson for us. When we believe our spouse has done something that is wrong, a grace-filled heart will not inflict immediate punishment, but will carefully consider the most merciful and loving options. Besides, I (Doug) can't even count the number of times I judged BJ as wrong, only to find out later she was right.

Before Joseph decided to accept Mary's story as the truth, she dealt with the possibility he might reject and expose her. Mary knew that the baby growing within her was ordained by God, that she was faithful and had done nothing wrong. Still, she had to cope with her pregnancy.

The virgin birth was a prophesied event, but dealing with the day-to-day reality of her unsolicited predicament was another matter. Mary willingly accepted the holy task in spite of knowing some of the inevitable consequences of claiming to be a *pregnant virgin*.

Joseph and Mary found themselves in an extreme situation that challenged their grace- and mercy-giving tendencies. The situation called for forgiveness and understanding beyond what most people are willing to give. God specially blessed this couple because they were grace and mercy givers.

The Chosen Have Servant Hearts

During their lives, it is likely Mary and Joseph were faithful in small things, then in progressively larger responsibilities, and finally God trusted them with one of the most significant and important jobs of all time. Through their ordeal, Mary and Joseph did God's will. They listened. God asked them to believe He would accomplish the humanly impossible through them. They trusted God and had a quiet and steadfast faith that was displayed through their actions. Mary and Joseph had willing and humble servant hearts. They received blessings far beyond what they imagined when they first heard God's call.

Do you have a servant's heart? Would you be willing to do whatever God calls you to do, no matter how small or large the task? It takes a humble heart of surrender to be a servant.

Receiving the Blessings

Joseph and Mary showed us that God chooses people who are morally pure, those who extend grace and mercy, and those who have servant hearts willing to risk all to carry out His plan. Why would we want to strive for such lofty goals?

Imagine this if you can: your two teenagers, whom you love dearly, ask you for the keys to the new family car. They want to double date to the prom (but *not* with each other, heaven forbid.) Your choice is between the irresponsible one who has many speeding tickets and a fender bender or the responsible one who obeys curfew rules and has a perfect driving record. Whom would you bless with your car keys?

Why would we want to be chosen? Because we would experience God's unsurpassed glorious blessings. Our heavenly Father will trust us with His car keys.

**The secret
to preparing your marriage to receive
God's special blessings is . . .**
Keeping morals, extending grace and mercy,
and having a servant's heart.

Accepting and Loving Unconditionally
From Doug's Perspective

Joe and Joanie had been friends since grade school. Then a tragic situation in Joanie's life transformed this once quiet, morally straight gal into one who began looking for love in all the wrong places, and they parted ways. Even her family disowned her for her promiscuous behavior.

Joanie ended up in a home for unwed mothers in Milwaukee, Wisconsin, in 1963. She didn't know the identity of her baby's father because she had experienced too many one-night-stands. One of the stipulations of being in the home was surrendering the baby for adoption right after birth.

Even though Joe had never been one of her lovers, his unconditional love for Joanie hadn't changed, even though she had. He was the one friend who still believed the best of her. He sent Joanie a letter like this:

"You don't have to spend a lifetime regretting a teenage mistake. I don't care who the father of your baby is. I would like you to consider marrying me and our providing a name for the child. I love you for you." Joanie soon left the home to marry Joe.

Marrying a young woman who is carrying another man's child requires an unusually large heart of acceptance and unconditional love. That also applies when new spouses have children from previous relationships. Both of these situations are modern-day examples of the challenge faced by Joseph and Mary. It requires patience and dependence on God for help and direction.

What to Do in Difficult Situations

Joseph was probably stunned by Mary's revelation. It would have been natural to doubt or distrust her. We don't know if Joseph had any counsel from parents, friends, or his rabbi. Considering the humiliation Joseph most likely felt, and because of the fact that he "was a righteous man and did not want to expose her to public disgrace," perhaps he kept the matter to himself. Rather than react to the news and do something he might regret later, he made a decision to carefully consider his choices.

Engagement at that time was tantamount to marriage and required a divorce to end the commitment to get married. After some thought, "he had in mind to divorce her quietly." When the angel revealed that God's Spirit was indeed the father of Mary's child, Joseph's eyes were opened to the way God saw his beloved.

What would have happened if Joseph had acted rashly and divorced Mary before the angel came to visit him? Joseph was wise not to act impulsively or prematurely. I have not been as wise as Joseph. In the early stages of our marriage I often reacted rashly to statements BJ made, rather than carefully pondering my response. I'm doing better. Remembering Joseph's story helps. When situations present themselves in our marriage we can take it to God before saying or doing anything rashly. This allows time for the Holy Spirit to speak to our heart.

Before the appearance of the angel, Joseph may have seen Mary as impure, deceptive, immoral. After the angel's appearance he saw Mary as truthful, obedient, chosen. Sometimes we see our spouse through the world's eyes, with a critical, judgmental view. God's eyes are full of acceptance and unconditional love.

Unconditional Love Today

Dave Roever served in Vietnam on a gunboat. A phosphorous grenade exploded near his head, leaving his face mutilated, with sight in only one eye. After treatment, he was given the first opportunity to see his new face. "When I looked in that mirror, I saw a monster, not a human being. My soul seemed to shrivel up and collapse in on itself, to be sucked into a black hole of despair. I was left with an indescribable and terrifying emptiness. I was alone in the way the souls in hell must feel alone."

After returning to the burn unit of a military hospital in the United States, he composed himself to see his wife Brenda for the first time since the explosion. Just before Brenda's arrival, he overheard another wife telling her husband she wanted a divorce. Dave expected the worst. As Brenda entered the room, he looked intently at her face to try to discern what was in her heart. "Showing not the slightest tremor of horror or shock, she bent down and kissed me on what was left of my face. Then she looked me in my good eye, smiled, and said, 'Welcome home, Davey! I love you.'"

Davey was the name she reserved for her husband when she wanted to express her deepest love and devotion (From *Welcome Home, Davey,* by Dave Roever and Harold Fickett.)

**The secret
to acceptance and
unconditional love is . . .**
Seeing your spouse through
God's eyes.

Saying Yes to God

From BJ's Perspective

Mary must have been amazed and confused when visited by the angel of the Lord and asked to do something that was beyond her realm of knowledge. She stood to be chastised, ridiculed, and perhaps stoned. How did she respond? "I am the Lord's servant," Mary humbly and obediently answered. "May it be to me as you have said." She is my role model.

Obedience Is Not Always Easy

As my 52nd birthday approached, so did the weeklong Christian Artists' Seminar in the Rockies. Annually, top Christian vocalists, writers, actors, dancers, and participants assemble in Estes Park to train, compete, and entertain at nightly concerts.

I fervently prayed, "God, this seminar offers training opportunities I've longed for. Attendance in the Drama Division could equip me to serve You better through my position as a church drama director. But participation is financially unrealistic."

Within the week, I received unexpected checks that totaled the sum of all the expenses! "Lord, I am overwhelmed with your generosity. You must have a plan for me since You provided these resources. What can I do for You?"

I felt an immediate response in my heart: *"Dance for Me."* How could this be? Dancing was a childhood dream because I was born crippled and contracted polio at age 10. Though my legs had since healed, the only place I felt comfortable dancing was in the privacy of my own home! "Lord, I want to be obedient but . . . *help* my unbelief!"

After soul-searching prayers and encouragement from family and friends, I packed a makeshift costume made out of old beige curtains and flew to Colorado. On the first day of competition, I discovered the other dance competitors were teenagers who seemed so accomplished, they must have danced their way out of the womb! Dressed in cute little outfits, they executed exquisite dance moves I didn't even know existed! I waited for my turn unobtrusively in the back of the auditorium, dressed in unfashionable curtains that unsuccessfully tried to camouflage my half-century-old physique.

The talented Christian professionals judged the competition and helpfully critiqued each competitor. When they called my name, I timidly stepped forward with pounding thoughts. "I don't belong here. I am way out of my league and comfort zone. I have to swallow my pride to dance for You, Lord. Please be with me."

As my music ended, there was complete silence. The head judge slowly stood up as I braced myself for a multitude of corrections, but her silence pounded in my ears. Eventually she whispered, "Awesome." I thought my routine was so bad that the judge's response was designed to placate this dancing granny who enrolled in her first dance class at age 50.

Then, all competitors were instructed to return daily to practice and sharpen routines and skills. I knew I couldn't take the daily embarrassment or frustration. With hot tears of discouragement, I returned to my room. I had aspired to be obedient to God, but it was becoming very inconvenient!

I decided it would be best to drop out of the dance competition altogether and attend the drama classes instead. After all, wouldn't it be more beneficial to hone my dominant dramatic proficiencies? I hoped God would understand that sometimes the things He asks are just too hard.

Again, I sensed a strong prompting: "Dance for Me."

It was a defining moment. I was torn, but I submissively chose to persevere in the dance division.

On Friday morning, during morning prayers, reflection showed me I had usually followed my own will and sought human approval. I finally comprehended the importance of seeking only God's will and approval. I prayed, "Lord, You have been so incredibly patient with me. I think I

finally get it. It's an honor and privilege to be here dancing for You! Is there anything else I can do for You?"

I felt an immediate response: *"Dance for Me . . . without
your wig."*

Horror struck my heart and I recoiled as if struck by a
rattlesnake. "I would feel totally naked and vulnerable
without my wig. Lord . . . *please* don't ask that of me.
Anything but that!"

Silence followed.

I had worn a wig for 17 years! Tumor surgery followed
by two heart attacks caused a reaction that made my curly
reddish hair fall out in clumps. The sparse ash-gray limp
hair that grew back was an embarrassment I hid. The
thought of going anywhere without my *cranial disguise* was
paralyzing. I hadn't even retrieved the morning paper
without my wig! Such exposure was more than I thought I
could bear.

Why would God ask the impossible of me all week? I
struggled with doubt until Proverbs 3:5–6 came into my
mind: "Trust in the LORD with all your heart and lean not
on your own understanding." I felt convicted. God had
provided this week of opportunities, taught me valuable
lessons, and guided me through the daily cutbacks to the
dance finals. He had proved Himself over and over. Once
again, I swallowed my pride.

Obediently, I removed my security blanket wig and
headed to the final competition. My naked humility made
it possible for me to focus solely on dancing for the Lord.
I put my heart into the expression of dance as a means of
worship. I had faithfully given God some of the most difficult gifts I could: surrender, obedience, and trust in His
perfect plan for me.

The competitions went smoothly for the 600 competitors in the different divisions. With a feeling of relief that my public dancing days were finally over (was it only a week ago they began?), I turned to leave. The head judge approached me to say, "Congratulations on a most inspiring dance routine, BJ. The judges have unanimously voted you the first place winner *and* the Grand Prize winner of all the competitions. You'll dance on center stage at the closing concert tonight!"

Tears gushed from my eyes. God had rewarded a crippled child's seemingly impossible dream of being a dancer. That night, a liberated grandma with "au naturel" hair danced in front of the other competitors and 3,000 spectators. It felt like I was actually dancing in heaven for God.

Acts of Obedience

By no means do my acts of obedience compare to what Mary must have gone through, but there are two similarities. We both chose to do what we believed God was asking of us even when it was "beyond our human understanding," and we both experienced joy beyond measure. In order to develop obedience, one must be willing to surrender control, self will, and pride. Obedience is the response God is looking for in order to bless us beyond our wildest expectations.

**The secret
of being able to say yes to God is . . .**
Having a surrendered heart.

Questions for Discussion and Action

1. When was the last time you had the opportunity to extend grace and mercy to your spouse? What did you do?

2. How might God's view of your spouse differ from your view?

3. How can you be more obedient to God? What is God asking you specifically to do?

famous lovers

Ananias and Sapphira

Acts 4:32–5:11

Holding Back From God
From BJ & Doug's Perspective

*A*nanias and Sapphira wanted to be known for their generous *giving*, but instead they will forever be remembered for *withholding* from God and the deadly consequences of this choice.

We learn God's plan for building up the church in Acts 4:32: "All the believers were one in heart and mind. No one claimed that any of his possessions was his own, but they shared everything they had." People willingly sold their houses and other possessions for the good of the church and for the benefit of all the believers. Barnabas sold his land and donated all the proceeds to support the newly formed church.

Along with others, Ananias and Sapphira witnessed Barnabas's generosity and the appreciation of the apostles and fellow believers. Were they jealous, covetous, envious of the attention given to Barnabas for such a selfless act? Did they want the same recognition? Ananias and Sapphira agreed between themselves to sell their land and donate the proceeds to the church but to withhold part of the earnings for themselves. That wasn't a problem. It was their money to do with as they wanted. The trouble was, Ananias and Sapphira decided they would say that they had given *all* of the proceeds while in truth they would only give a portion. Their hearts were filled with fraud. Did they lack faith in God's plan to provide? Whatever their motivation, they had agreed to lie. That angered God because He knew dishonesty would weaken the fledgling church.

God's Plan to Build the Church

When Jesus was with His disciples He promised them, "I will build my church"; "You will receive power when the Holy Spirit comes on you; and you will be my witnesses" (Matthew 16:18; Acts 1:8). After Jesus' death on the cross, the Holy Spirit came to dwell within each believer to help build His church. One hundred twenty believers first experienced a transformation through the indwelling power of the Holy Spirit. Soon their numbers grew to more than 3,000. "All the believers were together and had everything in common. Selling their possessions and goods, they gave to anyone as he had need" (Acts 2:44–45).

God rebuked Ananias and Sapphira by striking them dead. That teaches us God hates hypocritical, selfish, deceitful behavior. Examining their story gave us a new perspective. When applying the lessons learned from Ananias and Sapphira to our marriage, we see where we, too, have been guilty of *holding back* from God. It may be holding back our time, financial resources, or gifts and talents. We get caught up in our own personal agenda of daily living.

We are convicted of giving less to needy charities because we wanted to spend our money in our own way.

We have had enough money to buy ourselves a meal yet didn't contribute time or money to the local soup kitchen. We have declined service opportunities at church because we were too busy with our own activities. Forgive us, Lord. Holding back from God is a way of telling Him, "We don't trust You with the resources You have given us. We think we can handle them better than You. We want to be in control of them ourselves."

The Exchange

Gregg asked his wife, Lindsey, to return to him the cheap string of pearls he had won for her at the carnival when they dated. Lindsey shook her head no and held fast to the inexpensive costume jewelry she wore daily. Month after month, Gregg lovingly requested she take off the fake pearl necklace and give it back to him. Time after time, she refused to part with it.

Finally one day, Lindsey hesitantly and begrudgingly gave in to Gregg's persistent appeals. She slowly removed the sentimental keepsake and handed it to her hubby. He put the fake necklace in a blue velvet box next to a price-less string of genuine pearls and handed her the box.

We are so like Lindsey when we hold back our time, talent, or resources from God. Does God hear us saying we don't trust Him with our life? What does God think when we cling so desperately to worldliness? God has priceless pearls to give us when we totally trust Him.

> **The secret
> of being generous with God is . . .**
> Remembering how generous God is with you,
> and reciprocating with your time, talent,
> and treasures.

Accountability Pays Dividends

From Doug's Perspective

The Scripture states that Ananias lied to God and Sapphira tested the Holy Spirit, but it gives no direct reason for God's decision to strike them dead because of it. Perhaps a point was being made about the importance of being honest with God. Just ask Jesus how much He dislikes hypocrisy (Matthew 23). Or perhaps God was showing that selfishness in the church would result in the death of the church. Or maybe it was because the church is the body of Christ, and Jesus said, "If your right eye causes you to sin, gouge it out and throw it away. It is better for you to lose one part of your body than for your whole body to be thrown into hell" (Matthew 5:29).

Whatever the reason, Ananias's sin and its consequences could have been prevented. Too often we make
sinful choices because we are greedy, fearful, or weak. We
know the right thing to do but sin anyway. Hopefully a
spouse will hold us accountable to Scripture if we have
sinned or are planning to act contrary to God's Word. But
that doesn't always happen. Sometimes, as in this case
with Sapphira, our spouse consents to our sin.
Accountability with someone outside of the marriage is
so important for spiritual growth. "As iron sharpens iron,
so one man sharpens another" (Proverbs 27:17).

Because of their deception, God struck down Ananias
and his wife and both were buried together. Scripture tells
us, "Great fear seized the whole church and all who heard
about these events." No kidding! That's scary stuff. I
would imagine lying was not in vogue for some time after
that.

We all have weaknesses. Accountability will help
strengthen us in our weak areas. We can hold each other
accountable so a fate similar to that of Ananias and
Sapphira won't happen in our church.

Personal Accountability

A young father named Cody was a quality control inspec-
tor at a sheet metal shop and was new to our church. We
were paired for one-on-one accountability because I was
a little further along in my walk with the Lord. As accountability partners we met once a week to study Scripture
and talk about the challenges and victories of life.

One night he said, "When I approve a product, I sign a
form stating it meets all specs, so if it doesn't meet specs
I am lying. But if I don't sign off my boss may fire me, and
my family needs my income. What should I do?"

We searched the Bible for answers and found these verses: Psalm 51:6; Proverbs 6:16–19; Zechariah 8:16; John 8:32; and Ephesians 4:25. I said, "Now we know what God says about truth and lying in Scripture. We know that God promises to take care of us in all circumstances (Matthew 6:25–34). Do you trust God? If you confront your boss, he might fire you, but maybe God has a better job waiting for you elsewhere." We prayed and parted.

The next week Cody greeted me with an ear-to-ear smile. "I told the boss I wouldn't approve any more out-of-spec product. He looked at me real hard for a moment. My heart was pounding rapidly. Then nodded his head and said 'Okay.' I am so glad I did it. Now I don't have to lie any more. I gained more respect from my wife, my boss, and myself for choosing integrity."

Accountability in Marriage

I've got good new and bad news. First, the good news. Every marriage automatically comes with a built-in accountability partner. Now for the bad news. It's your spouse, the person who knows all your bad stuff, sinful ways, weak areas, and past faux pas. Not only that, it's the person you most want to impress with all your pure and righteous qualities. So how are you supposed to confess your sin and ask for help? I won't lie to you. It's not easy. But there is a secret that can help immensely. "Love your neighbor [spouse] as yourself" (Matthew 22:39). Confront and rebuke your spouse just as you would have your spouse confront and rebuke you: gently and humbly. BJ has reminded me by saying, "Did you forget you promised to take the trash out before the garbage truck got here?" instead of, "You didn't take out the trash again!" And she lovingly asked, "Did you intend to ask me before you bought that computer? Did you remember our agreement not to spend over $100 without the other's permission?" instead of, "I can't believe you would do that when I didn't agree!" We try not to blame, but seek instead to ask. We give the one who has sinned a chance to confess.

Try to avoid these stereotypes when confronting your spouse:

• The **Tattletale** will notice a sin but not say anything right away, waiting instead to repeat the matter at the most embarrassing moment in front of friends, relatives, or sometimes complete strangers.

• The **Boss** will demand a change. "Sinner, repent or face the wrath of God!" This style typically lacks compassion and is generally ineffective in helping someone recognize and deal in an effective way with their sin.

• The **Jekyll/Hyde** personality will not mention your shortcomings but will then attempt to punish you in some unrelated way. This is the passive-aggressive personality. For instance, if you have a habit of overspending, your spouse may not directly confront you but will punish you for your sin by doing something to get even, such as watching sports all day rather than going with the family on a trip to the park.

• The **Drill Sergeant** will not only address your current sin in a tirade of putdowns, but will bring up every sin you committed in the past six months, and perhaps some really big ones from years before.

It works best to keep these verses in mind: "Be kind and compassionate to one another, forgiving each other, just as in Christ God forgave you" (Ephesians 4:32). "He who covers over an offense promotes love, but whoever repeats the matter separates close friends" (Proverbs

17:9). "Be completely humble and gentle; be patient, bearing with one another in love" (Ephesians 4:2).

Being Our Best

Accountability is finding another who follows biblical teachings and will encourage you to be your best for the Lord. "The purposes of a man's heart are deep waters, but a man of understanding draws them out" (Proverbs 20:5). We all sin, but those who do not learn from their sin are destined to keep repeating it. An accountability partner helps us confront and remove sin. "Therefore confess your sins to each other and pray for each other so that you may be healed. The prayer of a righteous man is powerful and effective" (James 5:16). As we confess and deal with the sin in our lives, we become more like Jesus, making it easier for our spouse to love us and easier for us to love our spouse.

The secret of strengthening our resolve in weak times is . . . Accountability.

The Truth About Lying

From BJ's Perspective

Ananias purposefully deceived Peter and was struck dead and immediately buried. I don't know where Sapphira was when all this happened to her husband or why no one even told her he was dead and buried. I would certainly want to know if a similar fate befell my husband. I know I would have been prompted to be a quick learner! Three hours after her husband's swift demise, Sapphira also blatantly lied about the money from the sale of their land and was struck dead also.

God commanded, "You shall not give false testimony" (Exodus 20:16). The consequences of their choice brought on instantaneous and severe punishment. "And all liars—their place will be in the fiery lake of burning sulfur" (Revelation 21:8). Once again, that tells us how much God deplores lying. The punishment from Ananias and Sapphira's story puts the fear of God's reprisal in my heart. He deals seriously with lying when we don't repent of that sin.

True Confession

Andy and Raylene were confident God had provided an affordable larger dream home to replace their outgrown starter home. They had buyers for their home. Everything was falling into place.

On the day the papers needed to be signed and submitted to the mortgage lender, one obstacle stood in their way. The down payment for their old home wasn't due until the end of the month. Without that money, they didn't have the cash deposit for the down payment on the newer home. Relatives didn't have extra money to lend them, so they asked a good friend to lend them the money until the end of the month. The friend was happy to write a check.

When Raylene returned to the mortgage lender, he asked her to sign a document stating the money for the down payment was from a relative. What a dilemma. Raylene thought, *Should I lie and sign the form? Or should I be truthful, refuse to sign the form, and possibly lose the house?* She was struggling in her heart to trust God. The friend encouraged Raylene to say she was a relative. The mortgage brokers said the loan would not go through unless the form was signed. She wanted the house very badly. She felt pressured and chose to lie.

Conviction by the Holy Spirit was immediate. Raylene was miserable the rest of the day as she wrestled with the sin. Andy had no idea what had transpired while he was at work. When he got home that night, the bomb was dropped. Andy was surprised his wife would lie. They turned to God for forgiveness, for lying, and for mistrust of His provision.

20 Types of Lies

Who do you identify with? Sapphira or Raylene? You might say, "Well at least I'm not a scheming liar like Sapphira!" I tend to be more like Raylene and just *bend the rules a little*.

The truth about lying is, "A lie is a lie." My loving husband brought that fact to my attention early in our marriage. I asked him to help me overcome my tendencies to exaggerate for the sake of a good story. I could have had a t-shirt made as a reminder. On it would be imprinted: "There are at least 20 kinds of lies . . . bold-faced lies, half truths, insincere flattery, false excuses, false impressions, exaggerations, overstatements, deceptions, falsehoods, untruths, fibs, misrepresentations, suppressing the truth, slanders, stretching the truth, little white lies, gray lies, a truthful statement taken out of context with the intent to deceive, evading the truth altogether, and fabricating the truth." Then, whenever I was tempted to lie or lean in that direction, he could just point to my shirt as a gentle jolt to my memory.

A statement is either honest or dishonest. Period. Although we know lying is wrong, it permeates our society today. We rationalize what we say and do to suit our own prideful or selfish desires. Some learn as early as preschool years that it's okay to lie as long as you don't get caught. We live what we learn at home, through the company we keep, and what our friends and relatives let us get away with.

I thought telling little white lies, stretching the truth, or exaggeration was acceptable because that is what I learned. As a matter of fact, I didn't think anything was wrong with it until Doug showed me Scriptures that convinced me God detests the darkness of deceit (Leviticus

19:11–16 and Colossians 3:9–10). Our God is the God of truth and light.

I used little white lies and half-truths to protect others from hurt or to protect myself from uncomfortable situations. I learned that although using half-truths may have seemed more convenient at the time, it was harmful in the long run. When Doug told me to tell the phone solicitor he wasn't home, it was a half-truth because physically the lights were on, but mentally Doug was not home after a long day at work. The truth of the matter was, I was undermining my own self worth and values.

Learned behavior patterns created by lying can become habitual when left unchecked. Dishonesty will continue until one desires to change. When faced with the reality and negative impact of lying, I made a new choice. Would it be lying to say I never lie any more? The truth is I try very hard not to lie in any way, and Doug continues to help hold me accountable.

Instead of being dishonest, God is glorified when I face the situation, get in touch with the feelings that are triggered by it, and handle everything in an honest way. Honesty helped me avoid feeling guilty, suppressing undesirable feelings, having to remember who knew which story, creating more lies to cover previous ones, undermining trust, separating myself from others, shaking other's trust levels in me, devaluing myself, compromising my values and principles, and raising barriers.

Steps to Cure Dishonesty

Pastor John Schletewitz taught us in a sermon that if you believe you have a problem with dishonesty, there are five steps that will help eliminate it from your life:

1. **Admit to yourself a problem of untruthfulness exists.** Then, admit it to God and to your spouse and ask for help to overcome.
2. **Explore the root causes.** Was it taught? Is it a bad habit?
3. **Surrender your tongue to God.** "A deceitful tongue crushes the spirit" (Proverbs 15:4). Whether it hurts our spouse, family, a friend, or we spend years of feeling guilty, a lying tongue hurts the liar.
4. **Make restitution for past lies.** If this is not possible, start from this day forward to be honest in all you say.
5. **Correct lies immediately as they happen.** A humble heart will allow your spouse and the Holy Spirit to gently rebuke you and set your tongue straight.

   I gave Doug permission to help me when he thought I was stretching the truth. By questioning me (not in front of others, but privately) or calling me on a statement I made, I became more aware of when it was happening. Once I became more conscious of my habits in this area, I could catch and correct myself. Now, whenever a thought enters my mind to exaggerate, I am aware it is the enemy tempting me into old behavior patterns. I can ask for help to reject the temptation quickly.

Honesty in Marriage

If we ourselves are honest, we have an easier time trusting our spouse. If we are dishonest, we then distrust. Any dishonesty in a relationship undermines the foundation of trust. If we observe our spouse cheating on the income tax form, telling us to tell the phone caller we are not home, or lying to relatives, our trust level in them is diminished whether we realize it or not.

My former husband committed indiscretions. For years he accused me of adulterous behavior that hadn't even entered my mind. A helpful counselor pointed out that it takes a philandering heart to accuse someone else of that behavior. Because he was lying and cheating, it was natural for him to suspect that behavior in others.

Breaking God's commandment by committing a falsehood should not be supported, enabled, or condoned by a spouse. We do not have to lie for our spouse. Rather, we are called to confront and hold our spouse accountable for being dishonest. "If someone is caught in a sin, you who are spiritual should restore him gently. But watch yourself, or you also may be tempted" (Galatians 6:1).

Before confronting a spouse, it is wise to check our own hearts. Am I trying to catch my spouse doing something wrong? Do I have a soft heart of love or a hard heart of control and superiority? A heart check and prayer are advised before rebuking a spouse.

Appropriate Support

Oftentimes, people feel driven to lie because of unmet needs—needs for acceptance, for a sense of control, even for love. It is sad to think we would lie and cheat because our needs aren't being met. Discovering what our own needs are, encouraging our spouse to do the same, and then communicating them to each other may help to overcome some dishonesty in our marriages.

When I examined why I exaggerate the truth, I discovered my need to feel heard, validated, and important. Once Doug knew my needs and responded in love, these needs diminished. What needs do you have? Partners' needs may differ greatly. Use the following lists to help identify and discuss your needs and your spouse's needs.

A man may need:
(1) physical intimacy,
(2) to feel loved,
(3) to feel respected,
(4) to be encouraged,
(5) supported,
(6) looked up to, and
(7) appreciated.

A woman might need:
(1) tenderness,
(2) compassion,
(3) validation,
(4) encouragement,
(5) security,
(6) trust, and
(7) unconditional love.

I didn't know what my partner's needs were going into our marriage, so I asked. I thought preventative measures were easier to deal with than repairs.

Whether dishonesty is a choice, a learned behavior, a habit, or a result of lack of love and attention, we can make a choice to correct it. God's lightning bolt may not strike us like it did Sapphira and Ananias, but our marriages may be short-circuited if we don't make honesty a priority in every area of our lives.

**The secret
of honesty is . . .**
Being truthful in all circumstances.

Questions for Discussion and Action

1. What is it you withhold from God? Why?

2. In addition to your spouse, who will you ask to hold you accountable (a person of your same gender)?

3. Which of the 20 types of lying do you struggle with the most? How can you overcome that behavior?

CHAPTER 10

famous lovers

Aquila and Priscilla

Acts 18:2–3, 18–19, 26

Romans 16:3–4

1 Corinthians 16:19

2 Timothy 4:19

Giving Your Life and Marriage to God

From BJ & Doug's Perspective

Aquila and Priscilla are mentioned in four different books of the Bible. One was never mentioned without being linked with the other. They were passionate and diligent in working together for the Lord and giving of self. What enabled them to *become one* as a couple in everyone's eyes? We suspect it was because they gave themselves and their marriage wholeheartedly to the Lord.

Aquila and Priscilla relocated to Corinth from Rome and continued their trade of tentmaking. We picture them setting up shop at the end of the marketplace where one could find them hard at work every day but the Sabbath.

Business establishments frequently connect people with similar interests, as was the case with Priscilla and Aquila. A fellow tentmaker arrived from Athens. Discovering they had much in common, and because the traveler hadn't yet set up residence, they invited him to stay at their home. Their visitor was on an evangelical mission and the visit turned out to be a year and a half long! Their housemate was the apostle Paul.

Can you imagine the teaching and learning that went on while Paul lived with them? We aren't sure if they were Christians before Paul's stay, but their fruit showed they were definitely productive in the church after that time. During and after Paul's visit, Aquila and Priscilla's marriage took on new meaning, direction, and purpose. They became servant leaders for the fledgling church planted by Paul in Corinth, and extended their gift of hospitality to new Christians. They committed their marriage to God.

Why Relinquish Your Marriage to God?

Why would any couple choose to relinquish control of their life or marriage? It's a strange perspective in our society, an unpopular concept. The truth is, we don't *have to* . . . we *get to*. When we get to heaven, don't we all want to hear: "Well done, good and faithful servant! You have been faithful with a few things; I will put you in charge of many things. Come and share your master's happiness!" (Matthew 25:21)? As a couple we won't realize our fullest potential, greatest fulfillment, and grandest joys until we give our lives and marriage to God.

Daily, we can choose to be all that we were created to be and do, to surrender our will to God's plan. If we desire to reap the benefits of a productive and satisfying life now and forever, we need to live for reasons beyond our human existence.

It's a Choice

Ken and Pam Ingold knew early in their relationship that agreement was going to be a trouble spot for them. It has proven itself true throughout their marriage from more weighty issues like parenting to less important prefer-ences like where to eat dinner (actually, they have strong preferences in that area, too). In 1979, their premarital counselor recognized their propensity to struggle and drove the point home when he said, "After you are married and in the peak of lovemaking, that is not the time to decide what type of birth control you are going to use." They needed to come to an agreement on crucial marital issues before they walked down the aisle.

Ken and Pam agreed absolutely on three major decisions:

1. To personally surrender his and her life completely to God
2. To elect God as the CEO of their marriage
3. To follow God's will for their life's work.

Stepping out in faith and making God the main focus of their lives and marriage better equipped them to serve God, each other, and others. Because of their differences, they were surprised when they felt called to a *team ministry* in the areas of premarital and marital counseling. They found it was their strikingly different paradigms that better equipped them to empathize with couples facing challenging marital disagreements.

"Ministering together has humbled and raised the bar for us," say the two. "It has helped us recognize the unique and special relationship God has given us."

Ken admitted, "There are hazards of serving as counselors together, though. I can't even count the number of times Pam kicked me under the desk because I advocated something I wasn't doing a very good job of myself!"

One day, a distraught couple sought advice from Ken and Pam on the best way to plan a divorce. Ken and Pam shared biblical principles for marriage, lessons they learned from following God's plan for their own marriage, and pearls of wisdom they gleaned from one another. Because of Ken and Pam's wise and godly counsel, the bickering couple elected to stay together long enough to attempt to apply the suggested advice.

Their marriage began to thrive after giving their personal lives and then their marriage to God. They are a living testimony and beacon of light to other couples who want to transform their marriage into a joy-filled experience. Thanks to God working through Ken and Pam, this once distraught couple is now serving God in ministry together.

Blessings in Marriage

We have seen too many couples, including ourselves, forge into marriage with a mindset of "What's in it for me? What am I going to get out of this?" They consciously or unconsciously seek to *get* instead of *give*. We learned a more loving and humble approach would be to ask, "What can I bring to this marriage?" and "What can I learn from my spouse?" A truly loving partner surrenders all to God and takes on the role of a servant (Ephesians 5:21). A servant continually seeks ways to lovingly *serve* God first, the marriage partner second, and others third. It is in giving that we find the real blessings in marriage.

Have you ever thought about the purpose for your marriage? An even more important question is, "What is God's purpose for our marriage?" We interviewed several Christian couples, asking them what they believed was God's purpose for their marriage. Their answers were varied, but the number one response was, "To have kids," or "To raise a family." These were our least favorite answers.

What is your answer? Do you think answering that question is relevant? A Christian couple said, "If we learn

God's purpose, it gives our marriage meaning beyond ourselves, especially when times are tough and we don't feel like being together." Consider Proverbs 21:31: "The horse is made ready for the day of battle, but victory rests with the LORD." We can make all the plans we want for our marriage, but success rests with the Lord. If our plans are contrary to His, we may be disappointed in the results.

God tells us the purpose of marriage is unity. "And they will become one flesh" (Genesis 2:24). If we align our will and desires with God's purpose of unity and oneness (Ephesians 4:3, 5:31) then we can make choices and decisions toward that end. God wants married partners to realize their fullest potential, greatest fulfillment, and grandest joy through unity and oneness in marriage. Is that happening in yours?

God's Specific Plan for Your Marriage

In addition to unity and oneness, we believe God also has a specific plan for every marriage. If you are uncertain about God's specific purpose for your marriage, you and your spouse can:

- Get on your knees to pray for clearer understanding
- Pray for open, soft hearts on how to better surrender your finite will to God's infinite plan
- Read the Scriptures together. God's will is revealed through Scripture.
- Study a couple's daily devotional together
- Explore the possibilities with married couples who are mature Christians and have walked the road before you.

When we seek, we will find. In growing toward a perfect union we need to surrender our life to God, work toward oneness in our marriage, and focus on His specific plan for our marriage. And don't forget, God wants us to enjoy this process. When we serve Him with a grateful heart, God stands ready and waiting to produce good works in our lives far beyond our dreams and imagination (Ephesians 3:20).

> **The secret
> to marriage fulfillment is . . .**
> Knowing and implementing God's purpose
> for your union.

Serving Together—Teamwork

From BJ's Perspective

My job is to focus on the female of the famous lovers pair, but it is difficult to talk about Priscilla without linking Aquila's name because they were always mentioned together in the Bible. Priscilla and Aquila were a team.

In the seven Scripture references, Priscilla's name is mentioned first five of those times. That could be because she had the gift of teaching, a gift important to the newly formed church. Still, they were a team that worked together for the good of the whole.

Team Aquila and Priscilla

We learn the concept of team from these famous lovers. There are at least four ways Aquila and Priscilla worked together as a team:

1. Tentmakers. Growing up, Aquila was most likely taught the family trade by his parents. He in turn probably taught his wife, Priscilla, the art of tentmaking. They worked jointly in the tentmaking business, but most likely they were responsible for different aspects.

2. Supporters of ministry. With their earnings from making tents, they provided income to support Paul's ministry, Apollos's ministry, and their own ministries as well.

3. Missionaries. Aquila and Priscilla traveled together with Paul to teach the gospel and worked together as a team to set up new churches and help new believers grow in faith, love, and good works.

4. Hospitality. One or both had the gift of hospitality, one or both had the gift of teaching, but both entertained church study groups in their home throughout their married life. Christians were welcomed into their home in every place they settled.

Team Players

Doug and I have always shared an enjoyment of sports, especially tennis doubles. Each team member of a tennis doubles pair is equally important. They play different positions, but when one partner makes a point, the team benefits. In our dating days, Doug and I won a tennis doubles tournament utilizing our strengths. Wish we could have transferred that team mindset and mentality into our marriage sooner!

During disagreements, we thought one spouse had to be right, the other wrong. That mindset left us feeling separated much of the time. Instead, when we learned to think of ourselves as a team, no matter who was correct, we both won because we were on the same team. After all, we rationalized, if Michael Jordan made a basket, it was the whole Bulls basketball team that benefited from the points. This attitude helps to keep us connected during the enumerable times we are faced with conflict. We have two choices when we disagree: do we personally need to win the point or the argument and be disconnected with our teammate, or do we want our team to win and stay connected?

Now we utilize a team concept in almost everything we do. Since we were going to be in the game of life together, we decided to play on the same team! Now we think of ourselves as *Team Jensen*. We realized both team members enjoy a special and unique position in our marriage. We use our individual strengths for building up the team. Our team functions best when we acknowledge, encourage, and admire each other's strengths. Doug loves to work with numbers; he pays the bills and figures the taxes. I love to decorate; he gives me full rein. I like to cook but hate to clean up; he loves to eat and willingly cleans up to encourage me to cook more. Teamwork.

Our differences help us learn, grow, and become more complete as individuals. Respecting, applauding, and supporting those differences encourages their development and makes for a stronger team.

Other Examples of Teamwork

Discovering each person's gifts and talents will help the marital team function at peak efficiency and with greatest satisfaction. Use the special talents God has blessed each partner with. Here are some ways couples with unique talents work together.

Brad and Christy Fox. In preparation for conducting a "Creating Loving Relationships" couples' retreat, we invited our friends Brad and Christy Fox to be part of the ministry worship team. Both laughed and asked, "You mean you want Brad to lead the worship, don't you?"

"Not alone," we reiterated. "We want you to serve together to lead the worship sessions."

Brad is known as a gifted vocalist/ guitar player, and Christy has always sat in the audience when Brad sang.

"We don't get it. How can we lead worship together?" they questioned.

"Simple. We want you to serve as worship leaders by each using his or her talent and gifts."

Christy and I were Bible study sisters. Her gift of teaching was evidenced each Friday morning for six years by our group of ladies.

We didn't expect Brad and Christy to do the *same* job in leading the worship, just to lead worship as a team. We envisioned Brad leading worship songs and Christy handing out song sheets, reading Scripture, and giving a talk on how the Scripture related to the lesson. Serving together but performing different duties was a new and exciting concept to them. Once they understood our plan, they eagerly responded, "We'd love serving together as *Team Fox!*"

David and Jeanie Lopez. David has a passion for working with technical equipment, and Jeanie has a passion for *signing* praises to the Lord. She is a member of the traveling Love in Motion Signing Choir. He uses his abilities as the tech man for Love in Motion's concerts by making the CDs, playing the music, and handling the sound systems. They praise Jesus to the top of their fingertips as a couple. Totally different gifts—one on the front lines, the other behind the scenes—but they still make beautiful music together.

Harry and Candace Kuehl. Harry and Candace embraced the concept of team effort when they felt the call to start a seeker-friendly church. Harry is a gifted evangelist and preacher. Candace is a quiet, behind-the-scenes wife. She has a passion for children. When their church began with ten couples, they met in the home of friends. Candace never imagined herself writing or delivering a sermon and Harry didn't want to be responsible for teaching the children's Sunday school. But, synergistically, they served together utilizing their different passions. With the help of others, they built a thriving ministry in the north county area of San Diego that is attended by thousands monthly. Their very different gifts were used for one purpose: to build up the church.

Bill and Pam Farrel. Pam worked to support Bill through seminary. When he became a pastor of a church in Southern California, he expected Pam to be a housewife. Pam, however, felt the call to finish her education and become a writer and speaker. Bill was not a happy camper. They had a baby at home, and he was just starting to build a church family. How could she find the time to do three full-time jobs: pastor's wife, mother, and student? How could he be expected to reverse the roles and be the supportive mate?

God worked on Bill's heart and convinced him Pam was responding to God's call. He made the loving choice to support the development of his wife's God given gifts and talents (read their story in *Men Are Like Waffles, Women Are Like Spaghetti*, by Bill and Pam Farrel). Pam is now an award-winning author and travels internationally to speak to women's groups. Together they are best-selling authors and travel nationwide to share a couples' ministry called Masterful Living. What a *team*!

Similar Interests

Ken and Jeannie McCoy are gifted musicians and vocalists (she a talented keyboard pianist, he a guitarist). Parents of two, Gerry and Jeanette Moffett were once traveling professional vocalists. Rex and Connie Kinnemann are songbirds who are worship leader and soloist, respectively. All love music and are serving together in musical ministries in their respective churches. Some are directors of music, some vocalists in the choir. All make beautiful music together in their team ministries.

God has endowed believers with many different spiritual gifts, so that the whole body of Christ, the Church, works more efficiently. Marriage is designed the same way. God gives spouses different gifts, talents, desires, temperaments, and interests so that the marriage will be complete, not lacking any important part. We are called by God to *become one* by putting our different pieces into the marriage puzzle. The marriage is strengthened when we choose to use those individual gifts to build up the whole, using it for the glory of God (1 Corinthians 12:4–31).

The secret of a successful ministry as a couple is . . . Embracing your differences to serve together.

Re-creating the Perfect Union

From Doug's Perspective

God designed man and woman to complement each other, to grow together into perfect oneness. Adam and Eve's perfect marriage continued until sin entered the world and distorted it. If sin perverted God's plan for marriage, and we are still sinful beings, then why even bother trying to recreate the perfect union?

In one sense we can never be perfect on earth. "But thanks be to God! He gives us the victory through our Lord Jesus Christ" (1 Corinthians 15:57). "God made him who had no sin [Jesus] to be sin for us, so that in him we might become the righteousness of God" (2 Corinthians 5:21). "Therefore, if anyone is in Christ, he is a new creation; the old has gone, the new has come!" (2 Corinthians 5:17).

In Christ we are new beings. God sees us as righteous because of our faith in Jesus. Therefore, we have an opportunity to create a perfect union according to God's plan for marriage. That plan includes (1) *initiating* a relationship with God, (2) *imitating* godly behavior, and (3) *inviting* God to be the head of your marriage. Aquila and

Priscilla, an ordinary couple, are a good example of a pair of famous lovers who recreated the perfect union.

Aquila and Priscilla

Based on Scripture, we believe Aquila and Priscilla recreated the perfect union. Both were Jewish. Persecution in Rome forced them to relocate to Corinth, which became a blessing when they met the apostle Paul. Knowing Paul's propensity to evangelize, it is almost certain they were converted to Christianity by Paul, thereby *initiating* their relationship with Jesus. They *imitated* godly behavior. Aquila and Priscilla hosted and probably led church meetings in their homes in Ephesus, Corinth, and Rome, and they even left Corinth 18 months after meeting Paul on an evangelistic mission to Ephesus. We also know they risked their life for Paul on at least one occasion and apparently risked their lives for other believers (Romans 16:3). There is nothing in the Scriptures to indicate they did anything in a selfish manner.

Aquila and Priscilla *invited* God to be the head of their marriage. I wonder if Priscilla and Aquila realized that hosting Paul was like having a *living* Bible in the house. Paul was spiritual nourishment. The fact Aquila and Priscilla hosted at least three home church groups indicated that they took his example seriously. Priscilla and Aquila went on at least three missionary trips, and helped in the teaching of Apollos and other new Christians. Aquila was a very humble man, allowing his wife to use her talents and gifts at the forefront of their ministry together.

The most defining characteristic of their marriage was their decision to embrace life as a team and use their diverse gifts and talents to build up the kingdom of God.

More than any other couple in the Bible, they had grown into oneness.

God's Master Plan

God's master plan for mankind is unity! "And he [God] made known to us the mystery of his will according to his good pleasure, which he purposed in Christ, to be put into effect when the times will have reached their fulfillment—to bring all things in heaven and on earth together under one head, even Christ" (Ephesians 1:9–10). Someday all heaven and earth will be united, with Christ as the head. Our destiny is unity. God and Jesus are already one (John 10:30). Jesus prayed that the disciples would be one (John 17:11), that all believers would be one (John 17:20–21), and that all believers would one day be brought to *complete* unity (John 17:23). We are to become one with Jesus, one with our spouse, one with all believers, and finally, heaven and earth will be united under Christ.

If we desire to fulfill God's plan of unity, the most helpful instruction/ marriage manual we can use in the process is the Bible. Remember the marriage triangle from chapter one? As we move closer to unity with God, through prayer and reading the Bible, we will move closer to unity with our spouse. God made marriage an opportunity for growing toward oneness. And if a couple only gazes deeply into each other's eyes and does not look out into the world *together* to accomplish something beyond themselves, they will not experience the joy and fulfillment God has planned for all mankind.

Seeking God's Plan

Seeking God's plan and purpose for marriage will help give meaning, direction, and strength to a marital bond. It is a goal the *team* can work toward together.

It wasn't until we almost shipwrecked our own marriage with selfishness and self-seeking that we sought God's plan for our union. In 1988, after two years of struggling to adjust to married life (and not being very successful), BJ and I decided we were ready to discover what God's plan was for our marriage. We researched what the experts said made marriages strong (communication techniques, active listening skills, conflict resolution approaches, and intimacy building ideas). After a year of focused learning and intensive application of these ideas to our marriage, we began to grow toward oneness. We were beginning to fulfill God's plan for unity and oneness.

Through prayer, Bible reading, and God-led happenings in our lives, we felt called to start a ministry for couples. It was time to give back to God for saving our relationship and giving us the wonderful knowledge of His plan for our marriage. At first we were hesitant, thinking, "We have only been married three years, and the first two weren't that great—how can we start a ministry to couples?" But God lovingly, persistently continued to prompt us, reassuring us that He does not always call the qualified, but He always qualifies the called. Once we yielded to God's will for us to serve other couples, our passion for life, love, and each other began to accelerate. At that time we had no idea where God's plan would take us. Even now we are exhilarated by the exciting roller-coaster journey of marriage and ministry. Following God's plan for our lives has blessed us beyond what we ever imagined.

We never anticipated feedback from couples we've

worked with who told us:

"You saved my marriage!"

"Now we have hope again!"

"We owe our great marriage to principles you showed us from the Bible!"

We realize we are only the vessels of God's message to these couples and His provision of hope for their future, but what a gracious God who gives us the opportunity to witness the transformations.

Like famous lovers Aquila and Priscilla and other couples who are passionate about God and seek His plan, we find that He continually blesses our marriage, our family, and our ministries. If you don't know God's specific plan for your marriage yet, seek it by praying, reading His Word, and pursuing the godly counsel of pastors and mature Christians you respect. If you already know His plan for your marriage, we applaud and encourage you to faithfully follow it daily. We can all make a commitment to create God's Kingdom here on earth, one couple at a time.

In summary, God's master plan for marriages is for the husband and wife to become one, using their individual talents and gifts for the good of the team. God's specific plan is different for each couple, but whatever that plan is, it will include helping build up His Church. Finally, God's overall plan for heaven and earth is unity. Unity is achieved through surrender to God. As husbands and wives, our job is to surrender our lives and marriage to God and follow His specific plan. Only then will we fully experience the blessings and prosperity God has planned for us.

> **The secret
> of creating oneness in marriage is . . .**
> Discovering God's purpose for your marriage
> and putting it into action.

Questions for Discussion and Action

1. Have you given your marriage to God? Discuss this with your spouse. If you haven't yet, discuss how you can do this.

2. In what areas of your marriage have you become one? In what areas do you see a need for improvement toward oneness?

3. What is God's specific purpose for your marriage? How are you doing following His plan? What could you do better?